Also by SCOTT O'BRIEN

Kay Francis—I Can't Wait to be Forgotten (2006)
Classic Images Magazine—Best Books of 2006-Laura Wagner—
O'Brien has a way with words as he beautifully examines Kay's films. He
skillfully uses Kay's own diary to paint a picture of an independent woman
ahead of her time.

Virginia Bruce—Under My Skin (2008)
Daeida Magazine—David Ybarra (editor)—*Under My Skin* is a well
researched, tactful, and skilled examination into the tragedy of a talented,
beautiful and popular figure in film history, desperate to fall in love at any
cost. Highly recommended.

Ann Harding—Cinema's Gallant Lady (2010)
San Francisco Gate—Mick LaSalle—Scott O'Brien has managed to come
up with a thick, fact-filled, smart and very readable biography of this
enormous talent. Harding deserves to be known, and the public deserves to
know her.

Ruth Chatterton—Actress, Aviator, Author (2013)
Huffington Post—Thomas Gladys—Best Film Books of 2013

George Brent—Ireland's Gift to Hollywood and its Leading Ladies (2014)
Classic Images—Laura Wagner—One of my favorites, Scott O'Brien, has
written another excellent biography. O'Brien etches a fascinating portrait.
His sources are extensive and, unlike hack writers, O'Brien provides pages of
documentation.

Sylvia Sidney—Paid by the Tear (2016)
Sight & Sound—Dan Callahan—O'Brien has labored to find the surviving
people who worked with Sidney. Comments from these co-workers add
texture to her story. O'Brien's book provides welcome insight into the
jabbing toughness Sidney needed ... to survive in show business as long as
she did.

Herbert Marshall - A Biography (2018)
Stephen Michael Shearer (author of *Gloria Swanson - The Ultimate Star*)
I will read *anything* by author Scott O'Brien. O'Brien's approach to his
subject matter is concise and sensitive. With *Herbert Marshall - A Biography*,
the author has given us another landmark publication of one of Hollywood's
best loved actors.

ELISSA LANDI
Cinema's
Empress of Emotion

by **Scott O'Brien**

BearManor
Media

Orlando, Florida

Published in the USA by
BearManor Media
1317 Edgewater Dr. #110
Orlando, FL 32804
www.BearManorMedia.com

Softcover Edition
ISBN: 978-1-62933-631-2

Printed in the United States of America

Table of Contents

Dedicated to Caroline Landi Thomas

Fox Studio's glamour shot of their "Empress of Emotion" (1933)

Foreword

When Elissa Landi arrived at Fox Studios in the Fall of 1930, she had a résumé of nine films to her credit, over a dozen stage plays, and had written two novels. Writing was her real passion, but her acting career had been pushed forward by the likes of Noel Coward, Dorothy Gish, John Barrymore, and directors Anthony Asquith and Rouben Mamoulian.

Landi's recent success in Broadway's *A Farewell to Arms* (1930) inspired composer George Gershwin to rhapsodize that her performance was "a symphony of emotion." Fox did a spin on Gershwin's comment, coupling it with Elissa's mother's claim of being the daughter of Empress Elisabeth of Austria. Landi had to cope with the studio promoting her as Hollywood's "Empress of Emotion." She had reason to go along for the ride.

Elissa found it necessary to supplement the meager wages of her barrister husband, John Lawrence. Her mother and step-father, Count Zanardi Landi, also enjoyed a cash flow from Elissa's earnings. Elissa's niece and namesake, Elisabeth "Suki" Landi Sennett reflected in 2020, "Elissa ended up supporting the family."

After three years at Fox, came contracts with Columbia, then Paramount. By 1936, Hollywood's attempt to pigeonhole Elissa Landi into a successful box-office "type" had proven a disappointment to, what she referred to as, the "thick-headed skulls" (all male) who ran the studios. Then came MGM. The skull of Louis B. Mayer was the last straw. Landi left films to concentrate on the stage and lecture circuit along the East coast.

Many have the misconception that Landi abandoned acting at this juncture, to concentrate on writing. Over 40 more stage roles and as many radio credits through 1948, belie that assumption. A decade of performances and lectures in all but five states, plus a teaching position at New York City College, underscore the fact that Elissa Landi was one busy gal! Her life was cut short at the age of 43. The story that follows will surprise many, and inspire them to look within. Elissa revealed that music was part of her own equation for, not only acting, but connecting to the human heart and authenticity. Music also helped Elissa rise above the many personal challenges she faced. As an author, Elissa Landi nudged her readers to step outdoors and sense the earth's mysteries, and be, as she put it, "polished by perception."

Introduction: A Daughter Reflects
by Caroline Landi Thomas

I never knew my mother. Her fame was such that most people thought *they* did. She was a movie star and, as my father repeatedly told me, one of the most beautiful women in this part of the world. Judging from the myriad photographs and films I've seen over the years, I certainly understand his opinion.

People imagined because I could talk a little by the time she vanished, I would remember her. Well in a way, I do. I also remember the layout of our home in Kingston, N.Y., especially the dining room table - probably because I like to eat. This was a stable table, long, narrow, heavy, probably made of oak. The times that my mother was with us and not off acting in one theatre or another, I remember she sat at the head of this table - or maybe it was the foot. I know I sat on her right. Although I sat next to her, I don't remember looking into her eyes or hearing her voice. I remember, clearly, her *not* being at home. I know I missed her, and I looked around for her the way someone older searches for a precious object they feel responsible for having lost.

It was a large household, and sometimes, when my parents could afford it, we had a cook. Her name was Anna Shillinger. My mother was Austrian, so she and Anna always spoke German while they were removing food from the steaming pots on the stove and ladling it into the serving dishes. I was in the middle of all this. I was hell-bent to stick close to my mother, because during those early days I felt I was physically part of her.

Writing was mother's passion. One of the reasons she had left Hollywood was so she would have more time for writing. However, it didn't work out that way. She was most always on tour. As star of the show, her presence was required for most of the rehearsals and then six days a week, twice on Wednesdays and Saturdays, for the duration of the run. If it was summer she might be off rehearsing at the nearby Woodstock Playhouse, which still exists and is one of the most famous summer theaters in this country.

I am reminded of a very curious story my father told me involving my mother, me, and my occasional baby-sitter Rudy Tronto. Rudy was in his teens, and later became a professional choreographer and a well-known director of musicals (*Sugar Babies*). He often talked about what an accomplished ballet dancer my mother was. She had studied when she was still a girl living in London, with a very famous ballet teacher, Serafina Astafieva, who taught some very, very famous ballet dancers such as Alicia Markova and Margot Fonteyn, whom I frequently saw perform, while I was studying acting at the Royal Academy of Dramatic Art. When my mother was a teenager, Astafieva told her that she had stellar talent and if she chose ballet as a career, she could become a prima ballerina. Obviously, my mother chose acting instead, but she continued to stay in form and used her gift for dance when plays and films called for it.

I'm sure I was four years old at the time this very odd thing happened. We had guests for lunch and afterwards we gathered in our large living room for coffee. Rudy had been asked to entertain us with his gift for ballet. He was having a bit of trouble with one of the steps, so my mother got up to help him. And in the middle of the step she stumbled. If Rudy hadn't caught her she would have fallen. There was an awful silence. And to cover it, I piped up with what I thought was a helpful explanation, "Mummy has died … ." And when the horrible silence got even worse, I added "a little … ," trying to lessen whatever was bad about what I had just said. After a moment my father made a little joke, or said something clever, and everyone jumped in and pretended that nothing had happened.

Well, it was obvious I must have overheard a phone conversation between my father and my mother's doctor - and somehow the tone of my father's voice coupling the word 'died' with my mother's name would have tipped me off that there was something wrong. That is why I had tried to explain away my mother's stumble with that particular word 'died.' Later, when I was already grown up, my father told me that he and my mother's doctor had decided not to tell her that she was fatally ill. And I'm sure no one in the room that afternoon had been told. But I have a feeling that everyone knew there was something terribly wrong with her, even though she was able to go on performing almost until the end. Her death wrenched us apart, but I had to go on 'living or partly living' as T.S. Eliot would put it. There's no blame here. Everyone did their very best to comfort me. It wasn't their fault nothing ever gave me the closure I needed.

All this happened at the beginning of my life. A lot of it has come back over the years. I still can't see my mother, but I can 'feel' about her at last. I've always carefully avoided knowing too much about her and all that I lost. I started to write about my mother's life, because Scott O'Brien asked me to. And I've written about her as accurately as a daughter can when she lost her mother at the age of four. I am the mother of two grown children - one is a writer and the other a Professor of English as it is taught to foreign students. I feel now as if I can imagine what it would have been like to describe my mother from the point of view of a daughter who grew up with her mother and continued to know her on into both her mother's old age and her own. And, I wonder if the feeling I have about my mother, now that I have finished the story, would have been all that different.

<<>>

I shall now turn my attention to the 'star' or maybe one could say director of this little essay. And that would be *ta-da*... Scott O'Brien, *drum roll*!! Finally here I am, already a grandmother, and a first rate biographer comes along to tell me so much about my mother I didn't know! First of all, he has done meticulous research. He's bursting with knowledge about her - many things that even I had never been told. He depicts my mother's fascinating life as a star, partnering an A-list of leading men, like her good friend Laurence Olivier, Cary Grant, Fredric March, Douglas Fairbanks Jr., Ronald Colman, and her love-interest (on and off-screen) Robert Donat. She was directed by Cecil B. DeMille in the most famous film she starred in - *The Sign of the Cross.*

Of course, the amusing and sometimes sad stories in this engrossing biography are firmly based on her character, her parentage, her friends, and all the famous stars and directors of that era with whom she worked. And one more thing, my grandmother claimed to be the daughter of the Empress of Austria - a story which my mother never discussed - neither denied or corroborated. Scott O'Brien's research is impeccable and perceptive. He sees her possibilities and how they went way beyond those that were offered to her. I'm particularly enamored with the way Scott tells the truth and yet he's actually asking big questions, giving my mother's life the genuine arc it had. He perceived the richness of her life, going much beyond what the facts give us. But while Scott embeds her in the glittering world of Hollywood and Broadway, he includes the subtleties of her inner life during those times, and the effect on her of the people who surrounded her.

One of Caroline's favorite portraits of her mother (1920's)

1946 - Elissa and Caroline at home in Kingston, New York.

Empress Elisabeth of Austria and Elissa ...
"incontestable proof" of a royal bloodline?

Chapter 1
Royal Roots?

Upon arriving in Hollywood in 1930, Elissa Landi was questioned about her mother's claim to being the secret daughter of Elisabeth, the tragic Empress of Austria. Landi declared, "I have no interest in proving the story."[1] When one veteran correspondent pursued the subject, Landi offered her a recipe for Hungarian goulash. "You can make it with beef," she declared, "but I prefer veal from the shinbone."[2] On another occasion, Elissa summed up her controversial connection with the royal House of Habsburg, by saying, "Who cares? Authors and actors have no nationality."[3] "I am living in the present ... not the past," she insisted. By 1938, her routine reply was, "I never comment on that."[4]

After filing for citizenship in the late 1930's, Landi commented, "It took Washington three years to decide what country I should renounce to become an American citizen. I finally renounced two of them."[5] Actress/screenwriter Elsie Janis barbed that Landi was "a composite of as many nationalities as the average Peace Pact." Tracing Elissa Landi's roots, royal or otherwise, is complicated by her own admission of relishing *invention*. The press often referred to Elissa as Italian, born in Venice, Italy, December 6, 1904.[6] In a

1

1932 interview, Landi revealed, "My birthplace was Venice, Italy; and the fact that the records were destroyed by fire, leaves me strangely unmoved."[7] When filling out her biography for publicity purposes, Landi claimed that her nationality was English. Indeed, she had spent most of her life in England. However, her birth name Elisabeth Marie Christine Kuhnelt, is decidedly an Austrian extraction, as her father Richard Kuhnelt, was an infantry lieutenant in the Austrian Army.[8] Elissa's mother, the former Caroline Kaiser, also grew up in Austria. Their marriage took place in January 1902. Elissa's older brother Anthony was born that November. By the time Elissa arrived, the Kuhnelts were living in an old farmstead in Kleinhart, just outside Vienna.

In 1999, Martin A. Kelly, a fan of Landi's, came up with a logical explanation for the complications surrounding Elissa's origins in his biographical article written for *Classic Images*. Caroline's decision to claim Italy as Elissa and Tony's birthplace took place just prior to WWI, while living in England. Kelly detailed,

> Elissa was, of course, Austrian and to obviate wartime red-tape and protect her from anti-German sentiments, which were building, the parents [meaning Caroline, and Elissa's stepfather] decided to claim she had been born in Venice, Italy. This subterfuge became a permanent part of Elissa's pedigree.[9]

In May 1906, the Kuhnelts, along with the children's faithful nanny, relocated to Montreal, Canada. Kuhnelt found employment with the Canadian-Pacific Railway. In March 1908, Kuhnelt returned to Austria where he was restored to his rank of lieutenant. Caroline took three-year-old Elissa and her brother Anthony and headed west to British Columbia, and that was the last they ever saw of their father. "That's my *mother's* story," Elissa told American author Lee Shippey. "But—well, he deserted her. I grew up a child of the west. I was in Vancouver until I was nearly 8 and the breadth and grandeur and beauty of the west are in my blood."[10]

2

There was no money in those days. I can dimly remember my own mother—beautiful and only 24 when we went to Vancouver teaching languages under the name Mme. Francis so that we might live.

"Mme. Francis" purportedly tutored French and Latin.[11] Caroline also had a brief stint as a cook at the Yale Hotel, before she opened a small confectionary shop of her own on Pender Street, filled with Viennese sweets and cakes.

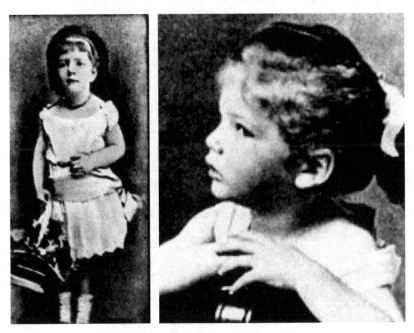

Caroline Kaiser as a child - Elissa at age of 2

During a lecture tour in the Fall of 1939, Elissa reminisced: "My first memories are of an old red-brown frame house in Vancouver where tramcars passed by and a hardy mountain ash tree flourished outside the door. Most of the time—I was then about four—was spent at the nearby sawmills chatting with Hindu laborers and Chinese coolies."[12] Pender Street was close to

Chinatown. A few blocks away was the harbor, where numerous sawmills employed Hindus. Elissa was described as "a wild little body" with a dual personality. When disciplined, she would bring "matters to a climax" by pointing a water pistol at the designated intruder.[13] "In the morning," she observed, "I was a tomboy member of my brother Tony's gang, and in the afternoon I was such a lady that I creaked, pushing my dolls around in a pram and teaching them in a perfect imitation of my mother."

Like her mother, Elissa's *favorite* pastime was inventing stories, which she eagerly related to her brother, a captive audience. At the age of five she ran away from home toward a schoolhouse where she burst into the principal's office telling him that she wanted to learn to write. "Our nurse used to read many of the Norse sagas to us," said Elissa. "I *had* to learn how to write stories of my own. It seemed I had so much to tell people."[14]

Landi never had any formal education until she was ten. "Yet at five I could read," she admitted, "and did. My mother acted as tutor." After Caroline read a Biblical account of the resurrection, Elissa's curiosity was piqued. "Is that true?" she asked. "Darling, I can't tell you that," her mother replied. "You must decide for yourself what you believe when you have studied the subject ... I must warn you that it is not always safe to take for granted that a thing is true because people believe it." Shortly afterward, Elissa was inspired to write a variation on a theme.

> I had finished a tale with the words, "So she died and her ghost arose from her body." "What do you mean by ghost?" asked mother. "Soul," I replied. I decided that the story of Christ was true because it was so beautiful. My mother taught me to figure things out for myself.[15]

<<>>

While Elissa began "to figure things out" her mother became involved with a well-to-do Italian nobleman: Count Charles Zanardi Landi. He

4

was born in 1876 in either Italy, or Turkey where his father was stationed as an Italian diplomat.[16] The Count had a number of trades: ship salvaging, engineering, and real estate investments. The *British Columbia Gazette* (1911) noted that Landi, a Vancouver real estate broker, had purchased acreage north of the city in the Cariboo Land District. Caroline never mentioned the Count's profession, but indicated that *she* had made "lucky speculations in land." Indeed she had. The *Gazette* also listed the names of Caroline Kuhnelt and Fanny Latzlsperger (Elissa's nanny) as purchasing property in the Cariboo District.[17] These transactions took place after Caroline sold her confectionary shop.

Vancouver's economy, fueled by the Canadian-Pacific Railway, was a haven for enterprising individuals that included corrupt mayors, proponents of a thriving opium industry, and American embezzlers. Caroline's Count didn't fall into this category, but he was indeed an enterprising soul, who kept an eye out for lucrative ventures. After learning about her supposed royal pedigree, he was adamant that Caroline lay claim to her rights to the House of Habsburg. Consequently, she penned a letter to Emperor Franz Joseph in October 1908.[18] There was no response. In December, the Count himself wrote a letter to the Emperor. Subsequent letters were also left unanswered.

In her version of the story, Caroline had to go to the United States to acquire a divorce from Kuhnelt. This left her free to marry Landi. The marriage, according to her, took place 1910-11. However, details of the Count's naturalization papers in 1949, indicate that he and Caroline were married in Vancouver in 1908.[19] It is interesting to note that Landi had arrived in the U.S. in December 1906—his final destination ... Montreal.[20] Had he and Caroline established connections prior to her relocating to Vancouver? It is plausible, and may explain why she would take her children 2800 miles West into unfamiliar territory, and be able to afford such a venture. In 1939, Elissa indicated that it was her stepfather's engineering work that had taken the family to Vancouver B.C.[21] Even so, when Caroline made land purchases in 1910-11, she used the name Caroline Francis Kuhnelt.

The lack of response from the House of Habsburg made Caroline all the more determined to be recognized as an Austrian archduchess. She and the Count decided to sail to Europe. Elissa and her brother stayed behind in Vancouver, left in care of their faithful nanny. It would be over a year before they saw their mother again, who later lamented, "What grief I felt at the moment of departure!"[22]

<<>>

(c. 1913) Trio - Caroline, Elissa, Anthony

Columnist Inez Wallace aptly described Caroline Landi as "a big woman with a deep voice." This rather imposing figure arrived in Munich on August 28th, 1911.[23] Caroline had "secret" visits with Empress' Elisabeth's sister Maria-Sophie, who told her, "I know of the affair, but I believed you were dead." Days later, Maria-Sophie was begging Caroline to leave her alone, thus sparing her "grave annoyance." By October, Caroline was granted a second divorce from Kuhnelt, gaining legal custody of Elissa and Anthony. The Austrian Court, however, decided it would be too grievous for the aged Emperor Franz Joseph to meet the secret illegitimate daughter of his dead wife. Caroline indicated that she was offered a million crowns to keep quiet. She declined. During a sojourn to Italy, the Count advised Caroline that she should put her story to pen and paper. She spent the bulk of 1912 doing exactly that. It wasn't until August 1912, after Caroline and Count Landi had settled in London, that Fanny arrived with Elissa and Anthony.

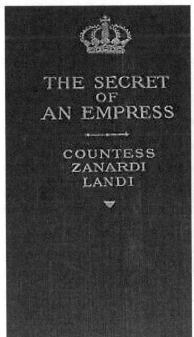

Countess Zanardi Landi

7

The Secret of an Empress

In 1913, Caroline's story was capsulated for London's *Daily Mirror*. Whetting the public's appetite prior to publication was essential. In *The Secret of an Empress* Caroline revealed that she was born in 1882 at Chateau Sasseteau in Normandy where Empress Elisabeth was staying incognito.[24] The Empress, age 44, did not want to submit her last child to the rigors of court life. The infant Caroline was placed with a family named Kaiser in Vienna. She was raised as their legitimate daughter, after Mrs. Kaiser faked labor pains to make this ruse more convincing. The Empress would make "secret" visits to the Kaiser home. Caroline's connection to the royal family was eventually revealed to her. The narrative refrains from indicating who Caroline's real father was, but she nudges readers into suspecting that it may have been the Empress's cousin King Ludwig II of Bavaria. (However, Ludwig, eight years Elisabeth's junior, never married. Personal diaries and letters indicate that his passions leaned towards other males.)[25]

The Secret of an Empress culminates with the Empress's murder at the age of sixty, by an Italian anarchist. Caroline was sixteen at the time. That was the gist of Caroline Landi's story. An epilogue detailed Caroline's marriages, her children (no mention of them having been born in Venice), and her pursuit to connect to the House of Habsburg. In *The Daily Mirror*, she claimed to have letters written by the Empress, but refused to release them. She determined that the "incontestable proof" to her royal bloodline was "the remarkable resemblances between portraits of herself, her two children" and the dead Empress.[26] In this respect, she had a point, particularly in Elissa's case.

Elissa made her own impression upon the press. She told the *Daily Mirror* staff, "I have 23 dollies and not one is ugly." They found her to be "a charming little person." A few weeks after the *Daily Mirror* revelations—bloody hell broke loose. Italy, prompted by the Vatican, halted the publication of Caroline's book. Adding salt to her wounded pride, Caroline learned that Austrian agents had asked Fanny to purloin documents from her. "But all in vain," wrote Caroline, "the poor woman was killed, being run over by a motor car." News items detailed that Fanny, 39-years-old, was crossing the road with the children at Marble Arch when a vehicle ran into her. She was taken to St. Mary's Hospital. Elissa and Anthony were knocked down, but not seriously hurt. They were also admitted into St. Mary's. *The Nottingham Journal* referred to the children's "miraculous escape."[27] Caroline offered no further details about the faithful Fanny, or the traumatic aftermath Elissa and Anthony surely endured in losing their lifelong companion.

A year later, Caroline opted for an English version of her story, casting aside plans for Italian and French editions. To celebrate the book's release, she and Count Landi married a second time on July 9, 1914 at St. Stephens in Paddington. Curiously, Caroline listed herself as a "spinster" and gave her father's name as "Joseph Kuhnelt."[28] From their home in Westbourne Park, the newlyweds eagerly awaited the release of *The Secret of an Empress*, by Countess Zanardi Landi.

Reviews were mixed. London's *The Academy and Literature* thought the book "remarkable and engrossing, if not a very convincing, volume."[29] New York critic Roger McIntyre, for *The Bookman*, mused, "Even the most unimaginative child ... replaces his parents with others of higher rank." McIntyre found Caroline's claims "less substantial than expected." Publisher George Putnam thought the story bore "an abundant evidence of unreality." *New York Sun* summed it all up as a "magnificent hallucination."[30] Other reviews echoed these sentiments. In 1915, a woman named Nellie Ryan, who was associated with a cousin of Emperor Franz Josef, came to Caroline's defense. In her book *My Years at the Austrian Court*, Ryan corroborates all of Caroline's claims. One critic of Ryan's autobiography offered, "You can believe as much or as little as you want," wagering that historians could "shoot holes through its 264 pages."

Prior to her book's publication, Nellie Ryan met with Countess Landi in person. Ryan mentioned that Caroline had "great ambitions" for her children. Ryan described Elissa, thusly,

She is most clever and amusing, dances [ballet] exquisitely and is already writing wonderful stories. Countess Landi ... is desirous that her little girl, whom she calls Mady, shall be a great linguist. Already she speaks French, German and English with perfect ease, and Russian is on the way.[31]

Ryan noted Mady's "great likeness to her dead grandmother." Meaning, of course, Empress Elisabeth. When Ryan asked Countess Landi to describe the Empress, Caroline sighed, "Ah, my mother's eyes were just like Mady's, so difficult to describe." When Ryan observed that Elissa's eyes were a very deep blue, Caroline volunteered, "My mother's eyes were really a deep sapphire blue, which in some lights seemed almost amber; and her hair was just the colour of chestnuts when they are lying on the ground." Ryan made brief mention of Anthony, "already very tall and handsome ... with a delightfully friendly nature."

<<>>

The visibility generated by *The Secret of an Empress*, allowed Caroline the notoriety and satisfaction of being a published author. Prior to the fall of the Hapsburg Empire (autumn of 1918), she set forth to create her next volumes, *The Royal Outcast* (1916), and *Is Austria Doomed?* (1916), the former she cautiously designated as Romantic Fiction. Following in her mother's footsteps, author Elissa Landi would one day wax enthusiastic about "the glory of living in a secret world, of one's own creating."[32]

Mady's passion for writing consumed her. In 1918, the thirteen-year-old completed her first book (unpublished), which she later regarded "far too ambitious in my choice of a subject. I entered the realm of the metaphysical and tried to write the story of one soul divided into two bodies."[33] She presented the book as a gift to her mother. "Mother was wise enough to show me the defects in my work," said Elissa, "rather than assure me it was wonderful."[34] By the age of sixteen, using the pen-name Elisabeth Zanardi Landi, Elissa's poem *Song of the Leaves* was published in the London magazine *Colour.* She had also finished a second novel, written in French. However, it took five rewrites and an interesting series of coincidences, before being published in 1926—in English. In the meantime, Elissa's life made an unexpected turn after she was caught doing impersonations of famous actresses at a London tea party.[35]

Teenage Elissa - writer and poet

Elissa and Tony - traveling companions

Chapter 2
"The World Was My Oyster"

"When I was a kid in England," reflected Elissa, "the world was my oyster. I could pick and choose. I could do what I like."[36] Elissa's oyster had many twists and turns in various locations. Prior to WWI, time was spent in Turkey where Count Landi's family had owned mines. The Count, Caroline and children lived six months by the Aegean Sea. They stayed with the Count's father, an interpreter at the Italian Consulate in Smyrna.[37] Soon afterwards, Elissa found herself in Bavaria, staying in a convent, where she befriended a gypsy girl. The two would steal away to a country inn and dance on tabletops to the tune of a peasant's concertina.[38] Sojourns to France, Switzerland, Germany, and Italy followed in rapid succession. Elissa and Anthony were perpetually riding the rails. In 1943, Elissa recalled,

> My brother and I spent much of our time on Continental trains. The procedure for our family was to arrive at the station early and to hurl ourselves into two unoccupied second-class compartments ... equipped with a variety of notices—in four different languages. In 30 hours one crossed three countries. My

brother and I would read these notices by the hour sometimes giving them the dramatic inflections we felt they deserved.

On the train between Calais and Geneva (I think it was the Orient Express) we pronounced solemnly:

Do Not Spit
Defense de Cracher
Sprucken im Wagen Verboten
Si Prega di non Sputari

The German version tickled our sense of humor—"Sprucken IM WAGEN." Spitting in the carriage! We felt this carried the implication that you could spit to your heart's content anywhere else on the train. The Italian translation baffled us. Literally "It is implored not to spit."

As we left one country and entered another we observed with interest how emphasis changed when it came to human weaknesses. What Germans took for vice, the Italians were inclined to disregard. When a German sign advised "Nicht Rauchen," (No Smoking) the Germans meant it. The Italians shrugged and lit cigarettes.

As for leaning out carriage windows, the Italians issued a mild warning. The French grew really serious. France was under-populated. The British, as always, formed a request: "Do Not Lean Out." (Implication: Don't be an ass. It's dangerous).[39]

Upon returning to England, Elissa witnessed the carnage of the World War. She never forgot the air raids and the sight of a shimmering silver Zeppelin brought down out of the London sky. Despite the chaos of the next four years, Elissa became skilled at the piano. The young adolescent continued her study of languages, tutored by a professor she referred to as "the awful Kate Murray" of London University. There were dance lessons from Madame Serifina Astafieva of the Imperial Russian Ballet, grandniece of the Russian novelist Tolstoy.[40] This idealized life was qualified years afterward, when Elissa admitted, "I am not an educated person. There was very little formal education in my life."[41] Brother Tony, on the other hand, was afforded the opportunity to study at Cambridge University, graduating with honors in history and economics.

<<>>

Count Zanardi Landi determined to raise the *Lusitania*

During the war, Count Landi was involved with the Royal Navy, salvaging ships. He later offered his assistance in resuscitating the British ocean liner *Lusitania*, which had been torpedoed by Germany in May 1915. There were rumors of large quantities of gold aboard. Even after Landi secured permission for this venture, authorities insisted there was nothing on board to justify such an expedition.

Things got underway in March 1922, when the Count and his brother Albert sank £70,000 into purchasing the salvage ship *Semper Paratus*. In 1923, after hiring 40 crew members, the expedition began in earnest. "We shall probably make a million out of it—perhaps more," he boasted to the press.[42] "The diving suit, which is my own invention, will enable divers to descend 500 feet." The ship would carry "equipment" to prevent usurpers from capturing the booty. Several weeks later, the *Lusitania* still remained in her watery grave. The *Semper Paratus* headed toward Belgium to locate a wrecked Dutch steamship that was assigned to a rival salvage company. Landi sent down his own divers, and ended up in a London court. The Count, who had failed to resurrect the *Lusitania*, defended himself by saying that his rival didn't have the ability to succeed.[43]

The fate of the *Semper Paratus* is rather curious. In November 1924, she sailed into the Black Sea where the Count rescued a stranded British steamer. Feeling he wasn't properly reimbursed for his efforts, he seized another steamer owned by the same company, ran up his own flag, and was charged with piracy. An out of court settlement was finally agreed upon. Count Landi bragged about being the last person convicted of piracy in England. He loved telling about the incident, which garnered him the nickname "Pi."[44] Elissa waxed poetic about her stepfather. "Ah, he is a dear!" she sighed to an American journalist in 1934. "I can say that because there is no blood relationship. He taught me to ride and he taught me to love Italy and art and history. He has been a great and delightful influence in my life."[45]

<< >>

About to take London by storm

Following the *Lusitania* debacle, Elissa began playing repertory. This was after Mrs. James B. Fagan (wife of the Irish producer) saw Elissa impersonate (unspecified) famous actresses at a London tea party. Mr. Fagan, also in attendance, was director at the Oxford Playhouse, then in its second season. Elissa was mostly interested in getting her first novel published, but the theatrical opportunity intrigued her. She wanted to write plays. "It was really to continue my writing that I went on the stage," she would admit. "I wanted to learn play writing and thought the easiest way would be to get right in the midst of acting."[46]

Elissa later revealed, "When I was twelve years old I saw a movie about Joan of Arc and I had a secret desire to play that character myself. By the time I was sixteen the desire to do so was overwhelming!"[47] She was referring to

Cecil B. DeMille's *Joan the Woman* (1916). Ironically, it would be DeMille that offered Landi her most memorable screen role. Sadly, she never got to play Jeanne d'Arc, a character suited to her persona and penchant for the metaphysical. Elissa's debut with Oxford Players was in Arthur Wing Pinero's 1887 farce *Dandy Dick*. The play involved an anti-gambling reverend, who, in order to repair the church steeple, bets his minimal savings at the racetrack on "Dandy Dick"—a 10-1 shot, no less. Elissa (3rd billed) was the reverend's teenage daughter, Sheba. The reverend had a rather progressive slant which he demonstrated by naming his daughters after Biblical women with notorious reputations. Elissa's sister in the play was named Salomé.

Rehearsals for *Dandy Dick* took place in London. Prior to opening night in Oxford (April 28, 1924) Fagan transported props and period costumes via motor lorry from London. The lorry caught fire and everything was destroyed (including Fagan's collection of autographed first editions worth a considerable fortune). This irreparable loss could have easily fueled the delivery of Elissa's first line on stage, Act I-Scene I: "Oh, my gracious goodness, goodness gracious me!" Landi admitted that her feelings about making her debut were rather perfunctory. "All I had to do was say lines that I had memorized."[48] Stage fright wasn't part of the equation. Besides, she always had the comforting presence of her mother, who accompanied her to the theater. On days with matinee and evening performances, the Countess would graciously cook supper backstage in a "strange little kitchen."[49] Cast and crew referred to her as "Everybody's Mother."

Elissa indicated that she occasionally participated as an "extra"—submerging her potential talents into the ensemble spirit, with a new play every week. Also in the company, as producer Fagan's assistant, was James Whale, who went on to mastermind such classic horror films as *Frankenstein* (1931). Whale would also directed Landi in her pre-Code comedy *By Candlelight* (1933).

Reports of Elissa's "connection" to the Empress of Austria eventually surfaced, and she made one thing perfectly clear. "I am not going on the stage for that reason. I want to succeed on my merits and I wish the critics to treat me exactly as they would anybody else making a debut."[50] She got her wish. By June, Elissa received accolades for her portrayal in another revival, *Everybody's Husband*. One critic enthused, "Three people must have credit for this delightful production—Mr. J.B. Fagan, Mr. Maurice Besly for the music, and Miss Elissa Landi, the young actress who gives such an exquisite interpretation of the young bride-to-be. Her dancing, showing her abandonment to the craving for freedom is one of the most beautiful things in the play."[51] And from there, Elissa Landi was invited to make her debut at London's renown West End theater district.

<<>>

***Storm* with Hugh Wakefield**

In July 1924, Elissa was signed to play the title character in C.K. Munro's comedy *Storm*, scheduled to open at the Ambassadors in August. Playing the heroine of the piece, the mistress of a married man, was certainly new territory for the novice actress, who sported a fetching red frock throughout the play. The action took place at a hydropathic hotel in Yorkshire. Water cures were popular at the time, but these players were more interested in love triangles. It was Elissa's character who provided the candor and humor that exposed, as one critic put it, "the miserable ... shilly-shallying of the rest."

A review in *The Era* noted, "Miss Elissa Landi has undeniable charm and good looks and her handling of the part of Storm was fresh and youthful." As for the play itself, reviews agreed that the action was long, dull, and repetitive. "The only thing that mattered," assessed the *Sporting Times*, "was the London debut of Elissa Landi—who scooped the pool." The review complimented her personality, temperament, physical shapeliness, and "speaking voice ... mellifluous, with a winning tone." *The Sketch* echoed, "Her voice is clear and pleasing and her grip of the character shows that she possesses not only a keen intelligence, but a natural aptitude. Miss Landi has a future full of bright promise."

Elissa recalled, "I remember that on the first night when the audience called, 'Elissa, Elissa,' I thought they were hissing, and fled to my dressing-room!"[52] The play was a success and ran for five months. American producer Gilbert Miller cabled Landi to come to Broadway. She preferred to stay put in London and share the stage with Edith Evans, who theater critic James Agate had designated as the most accomplished of English actresses.

The Painted Swan opened in March 1925 at Everyman Theatre. It came as no surprise when Evans, in the title role, "scooped the pool," dominating reviews for her superb portrayal of a saintly woman in a miserable marriage. Elissa, as her precocious daughter, received barely a nod. Not to worry. *Daily Herald* barbed that a play about an "expensive family ... being witty about nothing" was also a cure for those envying the "idle rich." Following the premier, the Earl of Oxford hosted a supper party at his Bedford Square mansion—Elissa, her mother, and photographers in tow. A photo from this soirée for prosperous people confirmed the *Daily Herald's* assessment.

Earl of Oxford (H. H. Asquith) sits next to Caroline. Elissa peeks over the shoulder of Lady Oxford - (Asquith's great-granddaughter is actress Helen Bonham Carter)

‹‹ › ›

As Elissa prepared for her next role, she began to feel that the stage was now counterproductive to her ambitions as a writer. Her manuscript for the novel *Neilson* was now in the hands of her friend, author Michael Arlen (*The Green Hat*). Arlen, in turn, would bring it to the attention of one of London's foremost publishers. After a conference, Elissa was urged to complete her novel and they would publish it. While her mind was preoccupied with this task, she found herself in a sumptuous revival of the popular Oriental spectacular, *Kismet*, which took place in the harems of old Bagdad.

During a rehearsal for *Kismet* at the New Oxford Theatre, Countess Landi supplied cast and crew with pikes of French bread, tomatoes and *pate de foie gras*. While enjoying this tasty nosh, Elizabeth McDonald, in charge of costumes, waxed enthusiastic that Elissa was "absolutely un-spoilt." "I remember the first time she came into the dressing room," said McDonald. "Elissa looked around with wide open eyes, like a schoolgirl. She examined the dressing table, the make-up box ... and then turned to me and said, 'I do hope I shall not fail anybody in this show'."[53]

In the role of Marsinah, the daughter of a thieving beggar, Elissa was adorned in exotic gowns and jewels. She finds herself in love with a common gardener, who, as it turns out, is none other than the Caliph, the Islamic leader. After opening night, one review said the revival "dragged at a funeral pace," adding, "I can only say that Miss Elissa Landi is pretty, but ineffectual." Aforementioned critic James Agate needled, "Elissa Landi is so pretty and so artless that her friends are perhaps justified in deeming criticism of her art to be irrelevant."[54] The play closed after only two weeks.

Elissa scanned the negative reviews of *Kismet* and decided to abandon the stage. After all, her dream of becoming an author was a *fait accompli*. *Neilson* had a publisher. Then unexpectedly, *fate* stepped in. John Barrymore, who was getting accolades for playing *Hamlet* at the Haymarket, was smitten with Landi's portrayal in *Kismet*. While in London, he telephoned her, "apologized for his presumption, and told her he regarded her work as marvelous."[55] Elissa was profoundly moved. She decided to stick with theater. Unwittingly, Barrymore saved her career. Coincidentally, James Agate had also taken a jab at Barrymore's Hamlet, saying that the actor occasionally robbed the Bard's words "of their just splendor."

Before being offered her next role, the twenty-year-old actress/soon-to-be novelist Elissa Landi was sidetracked by ... romance. The gentleman in question was a handsome, London millionaire stockbroker and art collector who resided in an historic mansion, and had a villa in the south of France. The announcement of their engagement took many by surprise. But, was it ... *kismet?*

Chapter 3
Movies & Matrimony

Teaming with Herbert Marshall in *Lavender Ladies* was a feather in Landi's theatrical cap. Opening at the Comedy Theatre July 29, 1925, Marshall played her novelist-father, whose best-selling books, unbeknownst to him, mirror the antics of his liberated daughter. She reads his books, takes a lover, and is determined to change the attitudes of stern, middle-aged "lavender ladies." *The Sketch* enjoyed Elissa's "zest" and "assurance." *The Tatler* noted her "sincerity of emotion which was very moving." Critic Harris Deans favored her emotional scenes, but cautioned, "Miss Elissa Landi has improved very much since her first appearance in *Storm*, but would do well to avoid those managers who would make her a star before she has studied all the rudiments of astronomy." And study, she did.

Elissa's decision to stick with acting, included coaching from Italia Conti, considered to be the best-known teacher of young actors in Great Britain. Conti had honed the thespian skills of Ronald Colman, Noel Coward, Gertrude Lawrence and Brian Aherne. No amount of coaching, however, prepared Landi for what happened next. Two months into the run of *Lavender Ladies*, she had a breakdown, left the play, and was ill for ten

Lavender Ladies (1925) (Caricature of Elissa with Herbert Marshall)

London (1926) Elissa's film debut (British National)

weeks.[56] Elissa also managed to get herself engaged. Before long she was endorsing Phospherine Tonic. "The roles I play are often very exacting," she disclosed in an advertisement. "I find Phospherine a really excellent tonic for counteracting the effects of nervous strain. I am never without a supply." The tonic promised a miracle cure for a long list of maladies, including: malaria, influenza, and something designated as "brain fag."

1925 Engagement to James Hart

Elissa's betrothal to James G. Hart, age 29, was announced at the end of August. His father was made a Chevalier by none other than the late Emperor Franz Joseph, husband of Elissa's purported grandmother. One news item referred to the love-match as "the third romance of its kind in three successive generations of the tragic Habsburg family."[57] It detailed Countess Landi's youthful liaison (mentioned in *The Secret of an Empress*) with a man of "relatively lowly station." It also touched upon Empress Elisabeth's sad romance with her cousin King Ludwig II. Royal bloodlines precluded matrimony for these ill-fated relationships. It was pointed out that Elissa "need fear none of the obstacles which barred the path to happiness of her mother and her grandmother."

The wedding with Hart, a London stockbroker, was scheduled for

December. As Elissa was not feeling well that fall, plans were postponed until after her comeback in *Blind Alley*, a play which promoted divorce law revision. Following the premier on January 4, 1926, a critic for *The Stage* indicated that the play itself needed "drastic revision," and thought Elissa "pretty as a picture ... but her emotional scenes did not ring quite true." By the end of the year, the same could be said for Elissa's feelings toward James G. Hart.

Any disappointment Landi had regarding *Blind Alley* was assuaged by the March release of *Neilson*. The protagonist of her first novel was a Londoner, a poet, and a philanderer. The narrative, as one review pointed out, focused on the "expansive psychological disclosure" of this gentleman as he falls desperately in love. Thrown over by the woman he truly fancies, the poet decides that his suffering will make a great artist of him.

Overall, the book was well-received. *The Sunday Times* nodded, "The style is uniformly brilliant." *The Daily Telegraph* concurred, "Her first book introduces us to a writer of considerable merit. It is an arresting piece of work." While on a lecture tour in 1941, Landi was asked about *Neilson*, and she deprecated, "... a silly novel, never worth much."[58] Even so, in 1926 it was listed among "The Best New Novels," encouraging Landi to push her pen forward and create her next book. In the meantime, she was sidetracked by the cinema.

<<>>

In April 1926, Elissa and fiancé Hart attended a banquet. At the adjoining table sat Dorothy Gish, who had arrived in London to make a film for British National. Gish spotted Landi. "We had never met," recalled Elissa, "but she came over and suggested I take a test for the ingénue role. I did and won my first part in a picture called *London*."[59] The director was the reputable Herbert Wilcox.

Running 61-minutes, *London* takes place along the River Thames, in the infamous Limehouse slum area. Gish, her virtue still intact, escapes the sinister clutches of the Chinese underworld. She has the good fortune to be taken in by a society matron whose dead daughter Gish resembles. Gish falls for the matron's nephew (John Manners) before, as one New York critic put it, "she is put in her place by a lynx-eyed society girl" (Landi). Audiences were also treated to glimpses of Gish doing the Charleston at the Haymarket's notorious Kit Kat Club. Curiously, this silent feature included a guest spot for America's Paul Whiteman and his jazz band.

In October 1926, *London* was released in the U.S. to mostly indifferent reviews, a reflection of the anti-British sentiment Americans had towards films made across the pond. The names of British players were omitted in the credits. *Film Daily* advised, "Dorothy had better come and play in her own backyard. Exhibitors will hardly find this suitable entertainment for American audiences." Brooklyn critic Martin Dickstein didn't mince words, describing *London* as an "insipid mess of blather." Dickstein mentioned the "absence of restraint" and "utterly terrible acting on the part of the English players."[60] Released in Great Britain in January 1927, the reception was similar, even though *The Sketch* praised the camera-work, as well as the acting of "the strong and clever cast."

London (1926) with John Manners (British National)

After viewing *London*, Elissa was not happy. "I looked so terrible that I quit," she admitted. She stayed off screen for two years. Later on she said, "I've solved the problem. I refuse to look at my films. I'm too afraid." *London* was fated to become a "lost film," now included on the British Film Institute's "75 Most Wanted List." Director Wilcox had better luck with his next feature *Mumsie* (1927), in which Herbert Marshall had the good fortune to make his film debut.

<<>>

When filming wrapped on *London*, Elissa did two plays back-to-back. In *Benediction* she had the role of a Reverend Mother who counsels a young Irish Priest who is conflicted about monastic life. *The Stage* pointed to the "cheap sensationalism" then summed up, "the wonder is that it ever came to be produced at all." In John Galsworthy's one-act satire *Punch and Go*, Landi played a young actress dealing with the temper tantrums of her producer. It lasted twenty-one performances. *The London Illustrated News* mentioned the "amusing interludes" and "pleasant acting." The real excitement took place off-stage.

News headlines detailed a robbery at the Landi residence in St. John's Wood. Heirlooms, jewelry, and a plate that had belonged to Empress Elisabeth were among the items stolen. A warrant was issued for a unnamed man, who had also taken clothing belonging to Elissa's brother Anthony.[61] In the aftermath, Elissa was in full gear to make her radio debut in a drama about a chateau being looted and ravaged by soldiers. The final scene in this WWI saga, *The White Chateau*, occurs when the family daughter (Landi), a war-time nurse, returns to the remnants of her home, and is resolved to rebuild.

After the broadcast, Landi got back on track with a *bona fide* stage hit, *The Constant Nymph*. This bold treatise on adolescent sexuality, focused on Tessa (Edna Best), a teenager who falls in love with a temperamental, married composer (Noel Coward). Also in the mix was her sister Antonia (Landi), who marries an art-lover, and is fated for a vivid if chequered life. Producer

Basil Dean, known as "Bastard Basil," relished the idea of reducing his cast to tears during rehearsals. As his plays were among the most successful, they put up with his sarcasm and abuse.[62] On opening night there were sixteen curtain calls. *The Sketch* summed up, "Undoubtedly it is one of the best plays we have had in a long time." *The Constant Nymph* ran for eleven months.

As Antonia in *The Constant Nymph* (1926)

Early in the run, Elissa caused quite a stir one evening. Noel Coward later recalled,

> I'll never forget the time in *The Constant Nymph* when Elissa Landi dozed off in her dressing room and missed her cue by five minutes. Cathleen Nesbitt was left alone on the stage stalking about like a caged tigress. In a moment of heroism, I went on

stage, just to give her someone to *talk* to. She practically threw her arms around me, and we spoke of the weather until we ran out of impending thunderstorms. Then I had a bright idea. 'Would you like me to play the piano,' I said. 'Please *do*,' she gasped. So I ran through a chorus or two, and suddenly there was a frantic banging and scuffling backstage. I knew it was Elissa—and she must have been in a real panic to get onstage, because she came bursting in through the *fireplace*! What an entrance![63]

Theatre magazine praised Landi's "striking performance." "Antonia, interpreted by Miss Elissa Landi," raved another critic, "seems to demand a play to herself." The only demand that Elissa made was a retraction from the publication *The Sphere*. The magazine featured a photo of her with an erroneous caption. On October 30, 1926, they promptly headlined a column, "Miss Elissa Landi." "In a recent issue of *The Sphere*," they affirmed, "we published a portrait of Miss Landi. We have just received a communication from this lady in which she points out that our statement that she was recently married is erroneous. We tender our apologies for the error."

Elissa's marriage to James G. Hart would never happen. In hindsight, it was for the best. Hart eventually tied the marital knot in 1930 with a wealthy young widow, three months after her elderly, knighted husband bit the dust. By 1943, Hart was expelled from the London Stock Exchange for breaching war-time regulations, after making a million pounds. "I deserve a rap on the knuckles," he conceded, "but not the supreme penalty. The government has taken over my London house, and all I have left is 12 rooms out of 49."[64]

Perhaps another reason Elissa asked for a retraction was that she didn't want to discourage potential beaus. One in particular would offer a proposal during the run of *The Constant Nymph*. Prior to this love-match, Elissa had the opportunity to be smothered with attention by the fifty-year-old veteran actor Robert Loraine ... and *not* in a good way. In April 1927, the duo co-starred for two special performances of Shakespeare's tragedy *Othello* at the

Lyceum Club. Proceeds would go toward rebuilding the Memorial Theatre at Stratford-on-Avon.

Loraine took the title role, and Landi played his wife Desdemona. The climactic moment when Othello puts an end to Desdemona, whom he believes unfaithful, had Landi fearing for her *own* life. During rehearsals, Loraine threw numerous tantrums over his wig and costumes, taking out his frustration while strangling Desdemona in bed. When Elissa complained that he was too violent, Loraine thrust a pillow over her face, and bellowed, "You mind your own business, my dear young lady, and I'll mind mine."[65] This confrontation no doubt alienated her from Loraine, and impacted their *live* performance. A critic for *The Stage* surmised, "Miss Elissa Landi ... was cold and unconvincing." And, understandably so.

<<>>

Landi's romantic inclinations during the run of *The Constant Nymph* leaned towards a young barrister named John Cecil Lawrence. He was frequently in the audience. Lawrence was born in Cheshire in 1902. His family resided in London's Belsize Park. John's law practice was located in the chambers of the Inner Temple, the center for English law. Elissa and John were in no rush to marry, but one incident that brought the duo closer together was their encounter with a ghost-like apparition. In 1932, Landi described the incident, which she still found baffling.

I was in London at the time playing in *The Constant Nymph*. Johnny and I were engaged to be married and he called for me nearly every night after the show. This particular night was very warm and we decided to go driving for the air. We drove along the Thames ... and we encountered heavy traffic ... suddenly Johnny turned off the main highway and stopped near a large house seemingly as deserted as the road which lead to it.

We were preparing to drive on when an eerie half-light swept across our faces and a voice said, "Didn't hear me come up, did you? You seem to be nice young people and I won't disturb you. But you musn't stay here." We could see him plainly in the moonlight with a shining badge on his coat. "Sorry if we have intruded, officer," said Johnny.

The policeman rattled on about dead bodies near the river. Landi described his monologue as "the gibberish of a maniac." Then he vanished from sight.

Then Johnny whispered, "Turn slowly and look behind you and tell me what you see." A large tree stood about ten feet from the car. Its trunk seemed lighted from within and apparently imprisoned in the heart of the tree was a tall headless and handless figure. From its long flowing robes I judged it might be feminine. The light faded and left us in pitch blackness. Johnny lost no time in starting the motor and switching on the headlights.

The next day Lawrence made a few inquiries and discovered that they had visited the infamous "H House"—noted for a series of horrible murders. Because of his legal connections, Lawrence was informed that the officer detailed to that area had not been anywhere near the house that evening. Due to the fact that they had no such knowledge prior to the incident and saw the same things, "Ghosts," emphasized Elissa, "were the farthest things on our mind. I am convinced that Johnny and I heard words that night which had once been uttered by a human voice. We saw manifestations of forms that had once lived. Merely to say the house was haunted is a lazy-minded method of evading the facts."[66]

After the ghost episode, Elissa was given *The Glimpse of Reality*, a dramatic sketch written by George Bernard Shaw. Landi referred to Shaw as "the most original writer living today. He always has something new to say." *The Glimpse of Reality* was scheduled for four performances in November

1927. Set in the 18th century, an Italian peasant girl named Guilia (Landi) lures Count Ferrucio to an inn. Her father will be rewarded a considerable sum by a rival feudal lord if he murders Ferrucio. For the first time in his hedonistic life Ferrucio experiences terror. Then, in one inexplicable moment, he recognizes his own humanity. The peasant-folk are so impressed that they abandon the plan for murder. Instead, they trade-off for simple blackmail, which would be more profitable in the long run. *Daily Herald* thought Shaw's play "a characteristically merry eye-opener." *The Illustrated London News* complimented the cast, stating, "Miss Elissa Landi was altogether delightful."

Elissa and husband John Lawrence (1931)

In the New Year, Elissa focused on films and matrimony. She and John Lawrence tied the knot at St. Marylebone Registrar on January 28, 1928.

Elissa, officially an Austrian, was finally a British citizen, and now going by Elisabeth Marie Lawrence. The newlyweds settled into Saint Edmunds Terrace, close to the beauty of The Regents Park. A week after the ceremony, Elissa found herself at London's Cricklewood Studios. They wanted her for a lead in the Napoleonic mystery, *Bolibar*. Still concerned about her image on screen, Landi insisted on five tests before she saw one that "almost looked like me."[67]

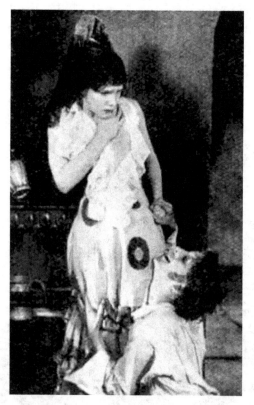

Bolibar (1928) (BIF)

Location shooting took Elissa about 30 miles south to Hampshire, where she and co-star Michael Hogan boarded a small boat. In a deep stretch of water, it suddenly sank. This incident was *not* in the script. "Miss Landi, who was the first to come to the surface," stated a news report, "cried for help, while Mr. Hogan sought to disentangle himself from the weeds so as to reach her."[68] Heavy costumes didn't help matters, but both managed to get lifted onto a barge. Landi was now prepped for additional location shooting in the Mediterranean ... that is, on the island of Malta.

Elissa was challenged with a double role—the promiscuous widow of a colonel, and an innocent Spanish girl, who resembles the widow. Three officers who fancied the widow, later turn their attentions to the young girl. The trio end up killing each other ... and the girl ends up stabbing herself to death. This takes place during Napoleon's Peninsular Campaign in 1812. When released in the U.S. (as *The Betrayal*), *Film Daily* acknowledged the "alluring camera shots" and "the acting of certain people in the cast." In 1987, film historian Ivan Butler praised, "Elissa Landi is radiantly right in *Bolibar* an apparently little-remembered film which deserves a better fate than total oblivion."[69]

Before filming wrapped on *Bolibar*, Landi signed with the young director Anthony Asquith, son of a former Prime Minister who was leader of the Liberal Party. Anthony himself was a staunch Socialist. For his debut as a solo director, he conceived the idea of filming a story with all the classes squeezed together, using London's subway as a backdrop. In Asquith's *Underground* (1928) we witness how the simpatico between natural acting, fluid camerawork (Stanley Rodwell) and lighting (Karl Fischer), creates genuine intimacy. Intrusive subtitles are kept to a minimum. Elissa, a shop-girl, meets two men on the subway who are complete opposites: a genteel subway porter (Brian Aherne), and a boorish electrician (Cyril McLaglen). Her choice an easy one. But McLaglen won't take "no" for an answer.

McLaglen persuades his ex-girlfriend (Norah Baring) to accuse Aherne of assault. The film's climax has Landi investigating this accusation, then confronting Baring, who ends up being electrocuted (!) by the sinister McLaglen. After a harrowing chase, McLaglen is apprehended. Landi and Aherne are free to follow their hearts. They make an engaging on-screen couple.

Film Daily rated *Underground* ahead of other British productions, adding

"Elissa Landi very natural as the shop gal." While *Underground* was considered a cinematic breakthrough for Landi, the real star was the London subway—the Tube, the routine bustle of rush-hour, faces of the everyday people—a regimented world of technological "progress." New York critic Creighton Peet put it succinctly: "The reason *Underground* is so effective is that never once has Mr. Asquith allowed us to forget the rush and push of perfectly indifferent passersby in the subway ... you may be eating your heart out or bursting with joy but nobody of all the thousands near you gives a whoop." The film was restored in 2009, with a vibrant new score by Neil Brand, and given a gala screening at the London Film Festival.

Underground (1928) with Brian Aherne (BIF)

<<>>

Earlier in 1928, Elissa was scheduled to be the first human face to be televised across the Atlantic to New York. Scottish inventor John Logie Baird helmed the transatlantic event, and wanted a "live" celebrity. He arranged for

Elissa to arrive on February 8th at Baird laboratories where the transmission commenced at midnight. Baird recalled,

> Landi arrived with her agent and we waited to hear from New York that our signals were coming through; we waited and waited, but something had gone wrong. I did what I could to console her with sandwiches and champagne, but it was to her a disappointing night. However, it enabled me to tell my friends that I had spent the night with Elissa Landi.[70]

The following night, signals were strong, but Landi wasn't available. Sitting under the glare of hot lights for hours on end no longer intrigued her. Later that year, Elissa transported herself (without Baird's assistance) across the North Sea to immerse her talent in Sweden and ... *Sin.*

1928 portrait by Howard Somerville

Chapter 4
Farewell to England

Prior to leaving for Sweden, Elissa graced the halls of the Royal Academy of Arts. In May 1928, Scottish painter Howard Somerville displayed his stunning portrait of her for the Academy's 160th exhibition. Landi was attired in a chic crimson gown (her favorite color was red). A London critic marveled, "I could have stood for at least an hour before the portrait of Miss Elissa Landi, but men continued to prod me in the back ... and step on my toes."[71] *Sporting Times* focused on Landi's "air of semi-mysticism." A viewer from Dundee concurred that the portrait stood out from the others, revealing an "elusive quality ... a vivacious young girl of today, with an elfin air all her own."

In the Swedish thriller *Synd/Sin* (1929) Landi suppressed her "elfin air" to be the doormat for an abusive husband (Lars Hanson). The film marked a return to the Swedish screen for Hanson, who had success in Hollywood playing opposite Garbo and Lillian Gish. Co-starring with a highly respected actor such as Hanson, was a career boost for Landi. *Synd*, based on the Strindberg play *Brott och Brott* (Crime and Crime), told of a Parisian playwright (Hanson) who, following success, prefers the arms of his leading lady to those of his wife Jeanne (Landi). He now sees their young daughter as a burden. Director Gustaf Molander does a capital job of capturing the tension of the married couple.

The cinematography (Julius Jaenzon) flows with atmosphere. After the daughter is reported missing, the climax takes place at a police station. The playwright and mistress, both accused of murdering the child, offer conflicting stories until the daughter shows up, unharmed. In the final scene Jeanne recognizes her husband's remorse, a victim of his own ego. *The Bioscope* praised the "sincere and artistic work" of director Molander, and "the fine acting of a very talented company." Another review enthused, "Miss Landi simply lives her part, and, though she is a young actress with her career before her, she will never give a better portrayal than this."[72] Her performance had staying power. At the 2013 Pordenone Silent Film Festival (Italy), *Synd* was considered "a triumph ... an unusual, wonderful film," and Landi was declared "the radiant Elissa Landi."

Synd (1929) Landi, Anita Hugo, director Gustaf Molander
and photographer Julius Jaenzon

Synd **with Lars Hanson (BIF)**

Cinema critic Lady Eleanor Smith, a close friend of photographer Cecil Beaton, wagered, "Elissa Landi, who, if she lived in America, would undoubtedly be a star of the first magnitude."[73] America would have to wait. Upon her return from Sweden, Landi headed immediately for the French Riviera where filming had begun for *The Inseparables*, a British film directed by Adelqui Migliar.

Landi played the innocent gypsy girl Velda, who is separated from her brutal guardian during an Alpine storm. A smuggler (French star Gabriel Gabrio) comes to the rescue, providing her shelter. A young Englishman (Pat Aherne), provides her romance ... until her guardian unexpectedly shows up. *The Inseparables* was praised for capturing the contrast between the majestic alps and the artificial glamour of Monte Carlo. *The Bioscope* nodded, "Elissa Landi plays Velda with grace and freedom, and well suggests the passionate nature of an untrained girl."

<<>>

Following her quartet of films, Landi returned to the stage for a satire under the helm of Canadian-born actor/producer Raymond Massey. *The Stag* ribbed wealthy big-game hunters who consider a day wasted if they haven't killed something. The action takes place at a Scottish Highlands lodge. Marion Temple (Landi), who is betrothed to Alan Cameron (Ian Hunter), has recently returned from Venice where she engaged in a romantic escapade. Filled with regret, she discovers that she is pregnant. The impregnator shows up at the lodge and offers her the address of a London doctor who can solve their "dilemma."

The Stag (1929) with Ian Hunter

While hunting in the Highlands, fiancé Alan intentionally shoots Marion's lover dead. Another guest at the lodge (Reginald Owen) claims to have pulled the trigger after mistaking the victim for a stag. Marion and Alan, who is willing to raise another man's child, walk away hand-in-hand. *The Stag* was bold stuff for 1929. *Britannia and Eve* called it "entertaining savagery ... stimulating and intelligent." *The Era* nodded, "Raymond Massey deserves praise for a very good production. Elissa Landi had some genuinely moving scenes." *The Sketch* agreed, "Elissa Landi was pathetic and sincere as Marion—she has made great strides as an emotional actress." *The Stag* was written by Beverly Nichols, chum of Noel Coward and Cecil Beaton. Nichols was part of Beaton's "Bright Young Things" whose outré behavior delighted the tabloids.

Landi then opted to tryout (two performances) a new play by John Van Druten. Van Druten gained notoriety when his first stage success, *Young Woodley*, was banned in London for two years by the Lord Chamberlain. *After All*, less controversial, covered a seven-year stretch of ups-and-downs in an upper-middle-class family. Landi played Greta, a cabaret dancer, who hastily marries the family son. Halfway into the play, one reviewer felt he had been watching the familial struggles "for a long, long time." The one bright note: "Elissa Landi was effective in her one short scene ... a most refreshing relief after so much tepid realism."[74] J.T. Grein for *London Illustrated News* also mentioned Landi's "poignant and magnificently acted scene." Grein, who had helped establish modern theater in London, recommended an overhaul for the play.

Although the Lord Chamberlain was satisfied, Van Druten made a note of Grein's advice and later a revamped version of *After All* opened at The Arts Theatre Club. *The Era* found the result "crisper and better-knit." In the new version, Elissa played the family daughter Phyl, which the review thought "finely acted." The same critic complained that Laurence Olivier, cast as the son, lacked the requisite "charm and gaiety." The following year, Olivier was cast opposite Landi in the film *The Yellow Ticket*. Elissa was admittedly captivated with him, and enthused, "He is the finest lover I have played

43

opposite."[75] Van Druten would emigrate to America, where his string of successful plays included *Old Acquaintance*, and the critically acclaimed *I Am a Camera*, which was adapted into the musical *Cabaret*. In 1943, Landi would star in a revival of Van Druten's comedy *The Damask Cheek*.

<<>>

Landi's second novel *The Helmers* (1929)

June 1929. At this juncture, Landi took five months off from acting to promote her second novel, *The Helmers*. One critic jested that the book was "as full of characters as Sanger's circus." The story focused on Valentina Helmer, a day-dreamer and mystic, living in Bavaria among the warmth of humble people. The "circus of characters" all fall neatly into place, as Valentina makes her observations about life. "Miss Landi's strength is her sense of character," wrote critic Oliver Way. "She also has a blessed quality of directness ... a gift for acute observation." Way included the following excerpt:

I feel there is a great deal of nonsense written about the budding breast and dawning womanhood, slowly waking, of young girls. Young girls, in my experience, burst into flower suddenly, over-night almost, like magnolia blossoms, both physically and mentally. Then they settle down, as if retreating into more compact maturity ...

"*The Helmers* is full of good things like that," concluded Way.[76] The *Yorkshire Post* assessed *The Helmers* as "an astonishing work for a woman whose chief talent has been expressed on the stage ... an unusual novel, subtly written."

Elissa and husband Johnny also had good luck in June at the Derby in Epsom. They were hosted by Irish horse breeder William Barnett, who begged the couple to bet on his racehorse, Trigo. Much against their wishes they wagered a small amount—a courtesy for a friend. Trigo was not considered a serious contender, at the odds of 33/1. Despite miserable weather and rain, the horse gained a clear lead early on, winning the Derby. There was very little cheering among a record crowd of a half-million people. The Lawrences walked away with $1000.[77]

<< > >

British author Elinor Glyn, known for her scandalous novels, had had her eye on Elissa's small feet. Glyn claimed they were perfect for the film *Knowing Men* (originally written for cinema's "It Girl" Clara Bow). Glyn produced and directed. Shot in the fall of 1929, *Knowing Men* made an impressive talkie debut for Landi. Glyn introduces the story while sitting in an Italian gilt chair. Waving her quill pen, she proceeds to answer the question, "What are men like?" She advises in a nutshell, that males can be cajoled by women who play on their vanity.

The plot unfolds inside a French convent, where young Korah (Landi) escapes the scrutiny of stern-faced nuns, to live with her aunt (Helen Haye) in Paris. Upon her arrival, the butler, the footman and the uncle are in hot pursuit before Korah has the opportunity to meet George (Carl Brisson), the man to whom she is betrothed. As the two had never met, Korah schemes (with her aunt's consent) to keep her identity a secret, introducing herself as "Collette." When George shows up, he is at once smitten with "Collette." The duo head off to a costume party modestly disrobed as Adam and Eve.

Knowing Men (1930) **with Carl Brisson (UA)**

At the party, Landi offers a tug at the heart as "Eve" experiences the wonder of her first kiss. "Adam" sees the beauty of her innocence. "Was that *really* your first kiss?" he asks, fully aware of the answer. While "Adam" deals with a conniving female serpent, the small-footed "Eve" sips her first glass of champagne before being dragged upstairs by a man in a monkey-suit. Predictably, "Adam" comes to her rescue. After a wild slugfest, a mix of breezy risqué scenes unfold until Korah's ruse as "Collette" is discovered.

Glyn's film was very much on par with Hollywood talkies of 1929. The co-stars registered simpatico, and Landi, at twenty-five, easily passed as seventeen-year-old Korah. *Bioscope* commented on the "sultry displays of sexitis [sic]," in *Knowing Men*, finding the "entertainment value considerable." A Dublin critic praised that Landi's acting was "natural and full of quiet mastery." *Close Up* predicted "a clean-up for exhibitors." Sadly, *Knowing Men* did not make money. Distribution in the U.S. was minimal.

In 2019, film nitrate specialist Larry Smith (Library of Congress) aptly described Landi's portrayal: "I thought Landi's strength was her innocence and playfulness. I loved the embarrassed glances to the side, as if she was caught feeling those stirrings that a girl with 'It' might feel."[78] In all probability Glyn was nudging Landi to become the British version of "It." She professed, "An actress like Elissa Landi knows instinctively what to do and does it. She is fascinating and intelligent."[79]

Hollywood would soon beckon

Landi was cast in Glyn's second British production *The Price of Things*, based on Glyn's 1919 novel. The film involved identical twin brothers, and one of them is engaged to Landi. When the groom is unable to attend his own wedding, the other twin steps in for the ceremony. The "fake" groom ends up falling for Landi, and vice-versa. An odd-mix of bomb-making, secret codes and Scotland Yard brought things to a climax. *Variety* summed it up as "hokum." *Bioscope* mentioned "the absurdity of the plot," but noted that Landi offered the "best performance." *The Price of Things* failed at the box-office. Glyn's productions were far above the cost of most British films. After financial losses (40,000 pounds), Glyn quit the British film business for good.[80]

< < > >

Prior to making films for Glyn, Elissa had signed on for *The Parisian*—France's first all-talking film. Adolphe Menjou was the star. For Menjou it was all about the money (a life-long obsession). "I made sure that I would get plenty," he boasted. "My terms were $125,000 and 50 percent of the profits."[81] His passion for money had produced what he called "an unruly ulcer," which kept what was intended to be a six-week shoot in Paris, behind schedule.

Director Jean de Limur, who had just completed *The Letter* with Jeanne Eagels and Herbert Marshall, was at the helm of *The Parisian*. Per Menjou's suggestion, French and English versions were shot simultaneously. While Landi was in the English version, Menjou starred in both. On screen, Menjou and his lovely young bride (Landi) are just settling down, when his illegitimate son shows up in Paris trying to convince him that America's business methods are superior to the French. While Menjou falls for his son's attempt to save papa from bankruptcy, he suspects wife Landi of falling for the son.

The English version of *The Parisian* was released in August 1931. *Bioscope* thought Landi gave "a charming performance" in a "mildly amusing" film. *The New York Times* groaned, "*The Parisian* ... succeeds in being merely tiresome." *Photoplay* called it "twaddle." Even so, Menjou had made his money, and

48

was homesick for Hollywood, where he returned post haste. In 1934, he and Landi would team up again for *The Great Flirtation*.

The Parisian (1930) with Roger Treville (Pathe)

<<>>

Two years into the marriage of Mr. and Mrs. John Cecil Lawrence, Elissa kept busy volleying stage, films and travel. By all appearances their relationship remained congenial. Fact was, she was giving John $100 a month to keep his own career on track.[82] Their residence—an Italianesque flat at 45 Belsize Park NW3, part of the affluent Hampstead area, was shared with brother Anthony, sister-in-law Annie and their infant daughter, Elisabeth, Elissa's namesake. Motherhood for Landi was put on hold, though she frankly admitted, "I believe that the most important thing in life for creative and imaginative women—are children."[83]

Landi's final screen outing for 1930 was *Children of Chance*. For this, she was able to stay in London where filming took place at Elstree Studios. *Children of Chance* was promoted as a crime drama, but never takes itself too seriously. The film offers an obvious poke at publicity-seeking theatrical folk. At the outset, Landi's shapely splash in a public pool and glamorous entrance at the Excelsior Hotel provides a light and lively presence that holds the screen. As the aspiring showgirl Binnie, masquerading as Lia, a notorious artist's model, Landi gets to sing a torch song (which became a hit off-screen). *The Era* felt that Landi registered "a convincing portrayal" in a dual role. "She looks splendid and exhibits a fine voice in a specially written number 'He's My Secret Passion'." One deserved chuckle Landi gets takes place prior to a date with a man pretending to be a Hollywood agent. Dressed in an evening frock and pearls, a friend gasps, "When your John Gilbert sees you in *that* darling, 'Good-night Greta Garbo!'" Landi gives a tongue-in-cheek impersonation of the illusive Swede, replete with soulful glances.

The plot thickens when Binnie discovers that Lia is also a jewel thief! When Lia's ex-con husband (John Longden) shows up thinking that Binnie *is* Lia, he scornfully calls her "a two-faced little slut!" (censors be damned). Scotland Yard steps in to get Binnie's fingerprints, which brings an improbable plot to closure.

Elissa enjoyed making *Children of Chance*. "It is a great help toward more versatility," she said. "There was lots of work to do and lots of scenes to do it in. I liked making the picture intensely, though of the two characters I have to play, Binnie suited me the better."[84] Landi's irritable, tough Lia provides just enough contrast to the innocent, congenial Binnie. A Boston review said of Miss Landi, "the freshness of her personality saves the show from utter failure." A 2016 DVD release of the film, despite variable sound quality and a few missing frames, preserves this light and entertaining offering.

<<>>

Elissa's hit song *He's My Secret Passion* **(1930)**

Soon after completing *Children of Chance*, Landi received an urgent cable on August 5, 1930. Five days later, she boarded the *Aquitania* for New York. She had been asked to play the female lead in a Broadway production of Ernest Hemingway's *A Farewell to Arms*. The 1929 novel, a romance set against the backdrop of WWI, was Hemingway's first best-seller. "I am terribly thrilled at the prospect," Elissa told reporters. "I have never been to the United States before and shall be traveling alone." She qualified her statement, saying, "My husband is too busy to join me. I feel like an adventurer going out into the unknown." Indeed, Elissa's "adventure" coupled with notable success in *A Farewell to Arms*, would prove to be a farewell to England ... *and* her husband, in ways she couldn't have imagined.

Publicity shots for Fox

Chapter 5
Fox's Garbo

"I wish they hadn't done quite so much for me"
- Elissa Landi (October 1931)

August 15, 1930. As the *Aquitania* approached New York Harbor, Elissa was filled with anticipation. "I was so excited I grinned and winked at the customs' inspector and he grinned and winked right back."[85] She was struck by the innate friendliness of people. "England is so terribly reserved," she said, "and it did something to me. Made me crawl into a shell when I wanted to be— friendly!" For two weeks Elissa soaked in the excitement of New York until her husband Johnny arrived on the *Mauritania*. The reunited duo stayed at Hotel Algonquin, gathering place of Manhattan literati and showbiz elite.

Elissa kept busy with rehearsals in Philadelphia, where *A Farewell to Arms* was scheduled for a pre-Broadway run at the Shubert Theater. On September 15, a standing-room-only crowd awaited the tryout of Laurence Stallings' stage adaptation of Hemingway's masterpiece. The following day, the

Philadelphia Board of Theatre Control were demanding cuts ... "to observe the normal decencies."[86] While audiences enjoyed scenes that captured undiluted Hemingway, censors felt the play's candor regarding sex and anatomy crossed the line.

Producer Al Woods cut short the intended two-week run. Woods encouraged Stallings to "erase some of the bolder words," but Stallings refused. After all, Hemingway's book was inspired by firsthand experience. He was an ambulance driver in Italy during the World War, and hospitalized after receiving shrapnel wounds in both legs. A short-lived romance with his nurse in Milan had its own repercussions. In the novel, the nurse was rechristened Catherine. The male lead, Frederic, loosely based on Hemingway, leaves his unit when Catherine becomes pregnant. They escape to Switzerland where Catherine dies from complications after their son is still-born.

On September 22, *A Farewell to Arms* opened at Broadway's National Theatre to a packed house. Hemingway's profanity, or "plain talk," was in full force, and there were no apologies to censors. Meanwhile in Montana, Hemingway was on a hunting trip, eagerly waiting to hear about the play's reception. "Write me what the damned play was like," he informed his editor Max Perkins. Perkins promptly cabled back that the play "is not going well."[87]

The play's director, Rouben Mamoulian made the decision to hire Landi for the role of Catherine. In 1943, Elissa recalled her meeting with Mamoulian in London.

> I was very young, very serious, and very intense. I remember telling him that either I must have the script and study it for a week or two or that he must make allowances for what was bound to be an un-lessoned reading. I think he was a little amused, perhaps a little annoyed. He told me to go ahead and read. After a short time he turned away and looked out the window. I couldn't imagine what was wrong, but I learned later that I need not have worried. He explained that he didn't want me to know how pleased he was.[88]

Mamoulian cabled producer Woods and Landi's Broadway debut was *un fait accompli*. She enjoyed the role and the challenge. "Catherine Barclay is a wonderful girl," said Landi. "She has warmth, responsiveness, and sensitivity, and she isn't afraid to let her feelings be known." On opening night, audiences gave Landi's Catherine Barclay curtain call after curtain call. While praises for the play itself were muted, Landi's portrayal was invariably singled out. "Elissa Landi achieved a beautiful, courageous and truly moving performance," wrote Charles Darnton for *The Evening World*. In his review for the *New York Evening Post* John Mason Brown elaborated on what critics concurred was the highlight of *A Farewell to Arms*.

> The truest pleasure of the production is to be derived from Elissa Landi's performance of Catherine. Miss Landi … brings to it a proper beauty, a proper intensity and proper purity. She catches, and transmits, as none of the others do, the fluent staccato of Mr. Hemingway's writing. And she alone recreates his touching romance in theatrical terms that preserve its quality.

A Farewell to Arms closed October 11, leaving Hemingway to jest about the profusion of curtain calls on opening night. "They must have all been people who wanted to sleep with either Mr. Anders or Miss Landi."[89] Although *Time* magazine thought the two leads "ideally suited to the parts they play," Glenn Anders, as Frederic, received scathing reactions from most critics. Critic Arthur Pollock described Anders as, "a fidgeting, gushing, blathering mummer who … makes a monkey of Hemingway's plain and forthright hero." Pollock confirmed that Landi was "the perfect Catherine … it is she who gives the Hemingway quality, she who makes it touching. She has moments of gentle magnificence. There are no other notable performances."

Landi's understudy, Dorothy Claire, offered an insightful look into Elissa's response to "instant fame":

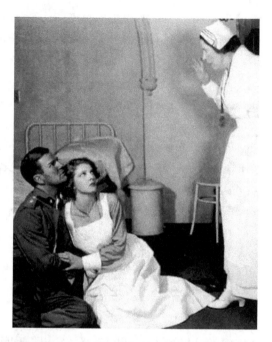

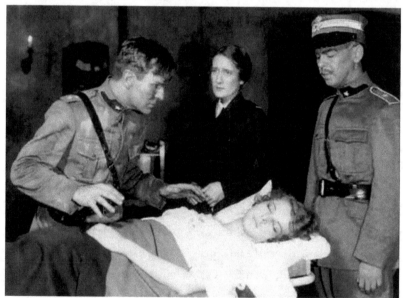

A Farewell to Arms with Glenn Anders

At rehearsal the whole cast could see how unusual Elissa was—so we kept warning her that no matter how well she played and no matter how much the audience like her, she would have to be satisfied with a mild handclapping. So, came [opening] night. Elissa was marvelous. She got curtain calls—twenty of them. The audience went mad. They stood on their seats and yelled, "Landi! Landi!" Elissa didn't know what to make of them. We had been careful not to let her expect too much. And the next day!

The next day there were telegrams, special letters, telephone calls. Film producers made staggering offers for her services. Elissa was afraid it was an American joke. She would pick up one of the offers and walk up and down her room with her hand to her head, saying, "What shall I do? What do they expect me to do?" It was hours before she could be persuaded it was real.[90]

Elissa was left to make her own decisions. After witnessing the flurry of his wife's success, John sailed home to London. It would be year before the couple saw each other again.

The burgeoning spiral of the Depression had affected several plays that season. Not to worry. Two days after the play opened, Hemingway received $24,000 from Paramount studios to film his best-seller. Landi herself received offers from three studios. "I knew I was standing at the cross-roads," she said afterward. "It was a terrific step to take. I confess I wavered. I was even more afraid of what pictures would do to my writing than the influence of the stage."[91] Following a screen test, she signed a three-year contract with Fox.

Landi headed to Hollywood, but missed the opportunity to play Catherine Barclay on screen. In December 1930, Paramount announced that Gary Cooper was assigned the male lead in *A Farewell to Arms*. Cooper indicated that he wanted Elissa to repeat her role, as he had seen her on stage. By the time filming got underway in July 1932, the studio handed Helen Hayes the role. While Hayes' unaffected style registered alongside Cooper's sensitive portrayal, she didn't receive the acclaim accorded to Landi in the

Broadway production. The film's highlight was the innovative cinematography of Charles Lang, who won an Academy Award.

<< >>

When Landi was asked why she chose Fox Studio, she explained, "Because MGM had Greta Garbo, Paramount had Dietrich and Fox ... " she gestured, hands held open. Production chief Winfield Sheehan, who had recently signed Humphrey Bogart and George Brent, wagered that Landi could fill the necessary stellar niche at Fox, christening her as the studio's "Empress of Emotions." Most likely, this moniker was inspired by composer George Gershwin who said of Landi, "She is a symphony of emotions. There is music in her every expression."[92] Landi received $20,000 for her first film.

Elissa mentioned her journey to the west coast and into the shrine of what was being referred to as "Tinsel Town":

> As the train chugged out of Albuquerque on its way to Los Angeles, I opened a day-old morning paper. I was on my way to film-city to seek my fortune, as it were, through the medium of American celluloid. Out of the page there leapt at me my own name coupled with that of Mr. Charles Farrell. In the next paragraph I found a quaint piece of contradiction: Elissa Landi was Fox's new Garbo. Odd, very odd. Didn't make sense.[93]

When she arrived on October 27, Landi took residence at the modest Vista Del Mar apartments. She and Farrell teamed for the WWI spy-drama *Squadrons* which became *Wine, Women and Sin*, which became *Body and Soul* upon release. She wasn't required to shoot any scenes until December. In the meantime Elissa studied her part, took long daily walks, and cruised around in her new Ford. More importantly, she began writing a new novel.

Body and Soul (1931) with Charles Farrell (Fox)

Body and Soul with David Cavendish and Charles Farrell (Fox)

Body and Soul detailed the failed attempt of American flyer Jim Watson (Humphrey Bogart) to destroy an enemy target. Watson dies, but his buddy Andrews (Charles Farrell) succeeds, adamant that Watson receive posthumous credit for the feat. Andrews then decides to return some letters to Watson's girlfriend Pom-Pom and relay the sad news. She promptly seduces him with liquor and passionate love-making. Andrews carries a naiveté about wine and women. He is unaware that the woman impersonating Pom-Pom (Landi) is actually Watson's young widow, Carla, who has her own reasons for not revealing who she really is. Andrews becomes infatuated with her. When he is told by another woman (Myrna Loy) that Pom-Pom is a German spy, he believes her, but not for long. Loy's character (unsurprisingly) was simply drawing attention away from *herself*.

London's *Bioscope* thought *Body and Soul* an "unconvincing story," but acknowledged, "Elissa Landi's performance as the disillusioned wife is one of the film's bright spots." *New York Times* admitted "the whole production hinges on the excellent portrayal of Elissa Landi." Cleveland critic W. Ward Marsh concurred, "Here is an actress. A woman of charm, poise, magnetism, power and intelligence. She leaves her supporting cast far behind her. Charles Farrell is no match for her. The screen becomes vital and alive when she is on it."

Following a 2016 Museum of Modern Art screening, critic Bob Lipton called *Body and Soul* "another ancient talkie ... Elissa Landi is very good in her down-to-earth attitude. Yet, dealing, as she must, with Charles Farrell, whose line reading is always overwrought, she seems a bit snide at moments." Fox had originally hired Bogart as Farrell's vocal coach, much to the former silent-star's dismay. Bogart wrote to his brother-in-law, "Charlie Farrell can't act worth a damn."[94] Landi herself offered Farrell tips on voice placement. Farrell, understandably, wasn't exactly pleased with either thespian's advice.

<<>>

Always Goodbye (1931) with Lewis Stone (Fox)

Elissa received top-billing for her second Fox feature *Always Goodbye*. Before filming began, she had a brief respite, as director Kenneth MacKenna was cruising off the coast of Mexico with his new bride Kay Francis. The film focused on Landi, a society girl named Lila, who runs through her inheritance, which costs her the adoration of several potential beaus. As a favor, Lila poses as the wife of a friend (Paul Cavanagh) who, unbeknownst to her, is a crook. They venture to an Italian castle near Lake Como where Cavanagh attempts to relieve a middle-aged millionaire (Lewis Stone) of his valuable diamond. Lila outwits the crook and falls for the millionaire. A mostly British cast fueled what one London critic described as "a dreadfully weak plot, but nevertheless amusing ... chiefly due to the acting of Elissa Landi." *Photoplay* placed Landi in their "Best Performances of the Month," along with Norma Shearer's Oscar-nominated role in *A Free Soul. The Era* deduced that Landi hadn't yet a fair chance to exercise her "undoubted abilities." MacKenna didn't make the grade as director, and Fox would eventually drop him.

Landi's next film, *Wicked*, was more of the same. In this 55-minute feature, as the pregnant wife of a dead bank robber, Landi endured imprisonment, then attempts to kidnap her own child. As for the film's length, director Allan Dwan argued, "I don't like things dragged out. People catch on, and it spoils the picture for them. It's better to get along with it." *Motion Picture*, none-the-less, rated *Wicked* "A slow-paced, laborious, melodrama filled to overflowing with suffering ... that will do no one connected with it any good, least of all Elissa Landi. No star, particularly a new one, should be charged with carrying material such as this." Spencer Tracy had the good fortune to drop out of the cast. *New York Evening Post* summed up, "If anything, *Wicked* is even more futile than [Landi's] other two pictures. With three such pictures in a row it is a wonder that Miss Landi has survived at all." Nevertheless, Cleveland critic W. Ward Marsh championed Landi's performance, saying, "Her histrionic gifts elevate the story not only to plausibility but to such emotional heights that you burn at the world's injustice to persecuted mothers."

Wicked (1931) with Irene Rich and Jacquie Lyn (Fox)

Elissa Landi WICKED Victor McLaglen FOX

Wicked (1931) (Fox)

Fox manager of foreign markets, Clayton Sheehan (brother of Winfield) indicated that by March 1931, they had received five loan-out requests for Elissa Landi. Unfortunately, she would have to wait another year before Fox relented. That loan-out proved to be a turning point in her career. Landi's next assignment, however, turned out to be her favorite role.

<<>>

Elissa offered the usual rounds of interviews. Ruth Waterbury, of the Hollywood Women's Press Club, aptly described Landi as "a strangely beautiful girl." "I talked to her just five minutes at one of those crowded press teas," said Waterbury, "but even that short time was enough to persuade me of her intelligence, her passionate absorption in her art and her very real sensitiveness." Landi herself was dazzled by the famous faces she encountered. "I have what you might call the fan magazine mind," she quipped. "The excitement of seeing Gloria Swanson is almost too much for me to bear. One day at luncheon I saw Marlene Dietrich at another table and my heart beat so loudly I could hear it. I think I should faint if I ever saw Greta Garbo. I never have, you know."[95] To prepare for this momentous occasion Elissa named her pet cat "Garbo." On a personal level, Landi indicated her favorite actress was Ina Claire, whose comic intelligence was focused mainly on stage.

During the summer of 1931, Landi purchased a home high in the coastal hills of Pacific Palisades (next door to Will Rogers, who was enjoying success at Fox with *A Connecticut Yankee*). She relished the Spanish Colonial architecture, an archway of trees and paths, and the feeling of sitting on top of the world. "I am a sun worshipper," she said. "I'm like a lizard. I lie in the blistering sun for hours, and I love it. I think best then. It seems as if the heat beating through me speeds up my mind while it coaxes my limbs to lie still. And it's a curious fact, but I have never burned at all." Landi indicated that she rarely went out, and occupied her spare time riding horses and finishing up her new novel.

Elissa described Hollywood as, "An entirely different planet. Like Mars. The Planet Hollywood!"[96] Journalist Constance Carr observed, "Elissa finds Hollywood artificial, adolescent and sophisticated all at the same time. But where all the orgies and 'Queer People' hide out she can't imagine." Over a cup of coffee during another interview, Elissa shook her head, "I keep seeing things in terms of scenarios. You know, close-up of a girl sitting down at a table. She takes a drink. Looks at a menu. et cetera." What she did *not* appreciate was the condescending attitude of male directors towards their female counterparts. "Auriol Lee," Landi indicated, "a woman stage director whom I admire very much, never drew an admission of her ability from any man in my hearing. Dorothy Arzner, the only woman director in pictures, did a glorious piece of work in *Sarah and Son*, but have you heard a male director praise it?" The film garnered Ruth Chatterton an Academy Award nomination. Arzner concurred with Elissa, saying, "A woman still has to be twice as good as a man in any field before she wins recognition, or even a chance."[97]

<<>>

The Yellow Ticket (1931) with Lionel Barrymore and Laurence Olivier
(Fox)

The Yellow Ticket (1931) (Fox)

Elissa's fourth feature for Fox, *The Yellow Ticket*, detailed corruption and anti-Semitism in Czarist Russia at the brink of WWI.[98] Adapted from a 1914 play, the film is enhanced with fluid photography (James Wong Howe) and robust direction by Raoul Walsh. We witness Marya (Landi), a young school teacher who, due to travel restrictions imposed upon Jews, succumbs to using a "yellow ticket"—a passport allotted to Soviet prostitutes. She is determined to visit her father, a political prisoner, who is seriously ill. She arrives in St. Petersburg and after being escorted to his cell discovers, much to her horror, his cadaver. As they escort her out, Landi's somber demeanor lets loose with uncontrollable rage, "You'll pay for this you brutes! You murderers! You'll pay!" She is stuck with her "yellow ticket" and the reputation that goes with it. Lionel Barrymore shows up as the Czar's lecherous Chief of Police. His overwrought performance makes him as sinister as he is absurd. Boris Karloff (prior to his success in *Frankenstein*) shows up, to better advantage, as a drunken Cossack who tries to molest Landi. At this juncture, she teams with a British reporter (Laurence Olivier) to give an inside scoop on the *real* Russia. "I should imagine there's quite a lot you haven't seen," she tells him, bitterly. The two fall in love. When Barrymore reads Olivier's scathing reports about Russia, he determines that Landi is supplying the details.

The Yellow Ticket **with Boris Karloff (Fox)**

Landi's nuanced performance as the virginal schoolteacher, fueled with determination, is a counterpoint to Barrymore's heavy theatrics. They match wits. She becomes *Tosca*-with-gun to Barrymore's *Scarpia*, in a drawn-out interlude that taxes the viewers patience. Olivier, in his second American film, was cautioned by director Walsh to underplay. He comes through unscathed with an easy-going sensitivity. In the dire situations they find themselves, Landi's emotional take makes sense, and Olivier's lighter touch provides some relief for the viewer. Marya's virtue is still intact when the lovers board a dispatch plane to make a narrow escape to freedom. Once they are airborne, the script calls for a dispensable bit of horseplay, before they embrace. The rapport between Landi and Olivier is genuine. When Olivier reminisced about *The Yellow Ticket*, he commented, "This, to my great delight, cast me as a leading man to my sweet friend Elissa Landi, a lovely girl and a good sort of actress."[99] In 1973, director Walsh divulged that after two weeks of shooting the film, Olivier "got hepatitis or some creeping crud, so we had to cut out a lot of his part."[100] Elissa used her own influence to assure Olivier's presence in the film. In 2020, Landi's daughter Caroline noted, "In one of my mother's letters, she mentions wanting to help 'Larry' get his career in America off the ground. And, *voila - The Yellow Ticket*."[101]

Following a preview, *Film Daily* praised, "Elissa Landi contributes the best work she has done since coming to America. Miss Landi is extremely convincing." Another review raved, "*The Yellow Ticket* has punch to it. But above all it has Elissa Landi ... who for the first time in her cinema career has been given a real story." Dallas critic John Rosenfield applauded, "Miss Landi is an appealing, sensitive heroine; a sure practitioner of effective dramatic technique. Her moment of confession to Mr. Olivier, the kind of sequence that ordinarily encourages a spectator to walk out into the lobby for a smoke, was projected with restraint and telling pathos." Rosenfield added, "We don't know whether you can call what Mr. Barrymore does by the name of 'acting.' It is a fascinating mélange of grimaces, and growls from the diaphragm." *Kansas City Star* scoffed, "Brother Lionel needs to tone himself down." In retrospect, Landi herself felt that *The Yellow Ticket* offered "the best screen part" she ever had—albeit while shooting retakes a soldier's bayonet inflicted a cut on her left leg, requiring several stitches. On September 29, 1931, her leg healed, Elissa headed for London, filled with doubts about Hollywood. A combination of publicity and lackluster roles seemed to be taking her nowhere.

Elissa with friend and co-star Lawrence Olivier

Playwright Robert E. Sherwood (*Idiot's Delight*) had great admiration for Landi. He felt that she deserved a "swift elevator" to stardom at Fox .[102] "She has beauty, power and skill, and a fine ringing sincerity," he wrote after seeing *Body and Soul*. Elissa sensed the repercussions of being a "Hollywood Star" prior to the release of her first Fox film. The key ingredient to her success in *Farewell to Arms* was the *lack* of publicity. People went to the theater with no expectations. Their positive response to her talent was of their own choosing. "I think Al Woods had the right system," she said later. "When I was rehearsing for *A Farewell to Arms* he told me that he hoped that I was not annoyed by the lack of advance publicity. He confided, 'Let them discover you themselves.'"

Landi's name came up in an interview with Bette Davis in 1959. George Arliss had advised Davis early in her film career. "At the beginning, when I worried about not getting my name in print enough," said Davis, "Arliss told me: 'Publicity is what follows if what you do up there is good. Never force it.' Remember the campaigns on Elissa Landi and Anna Sten? The publicity must not come first; it must come out of what you achieve."[103] Soviet actress Anna Sten starred in a silent Russian version of *The Yellow Ticket* (1928). Samuel Goldwyn brought Sten to the U.S. with the intention of making *her* into another Garbo or Dietrich. After a huge publicity campaign and three films, Sten became known as "Goldwyn's Folly."

Before boarding the *Ile de France* for London on October 2, Elissa met with a reporter for *The New York Sun*. Without being asked, she promptly offered her honest, if snide, assessment of Fox Studio: "I wish they hadn't done quite so much for me."

Fox's Garbo (by Ray Jones)

At home, holding her cat "Garbo"

Chapter 6
"Criminal Mismanagement"
& "Thick Skulls"

October 8, 1931. When the *Ile de France* pulled into the harbor at Plymouth, John Lawrence was there waiting to greet his wife, the "Hollywood Star." A reporter for *Bioscope* surveyed Landi at the posh Dorchester Hotel, surrounded by a crowd of influential pressmen as large as the one that greeted Charles Chaplin earlier that year. Her hair was lighter. Her teeth had been straightened. The gentleman of the press reflected:

> I contrasted her involuntarily with the quiet Elissa Landi of just over a year ago. She is changed. But only in appearances. Landi does not yet belong to any of the severely stereotyped of Hollywood femininity which we recognize so easily in all American films. Her own extraordinary personality has survived, and I believe will continue to do so. She is different, and when the

Fox executives have discovered exactly the kind of story to suit her she will be a sensation.[104]

The reporter voluntarily suggested "strong" woman roles. *Body and Soul* was finally being screened in London theaters, the ads screaming: "The English Star that America Acclaimed!"

While in England, Elissa had time to put things in perspective. Not only her career, but her marriage. The long separations from John weren't a major concern. "I never take my wedding ring off," she emphasized. "People in Hollywood amuse me, and almost frighten me. They are always telling me that my marriage won't last ... because we must be separate so much of the time. I think they don't know what love is. I would immediately divorce him if I felt that I dared not trust his love for me to survive a few months' separation. I don't live on companionship. I don't feel that my days simply must contain some devoted male."[105] "A few months" was a comforting miscalculation. It had been exactly a year since Elissa and John had seen each other. Another year would pass before the couple faced a series of difficult decisions regarding their long-distance marital relationship.

Fall 1931. Elissa and mother Caroline in London

One major concern for Elissa was her mother's health. Caroline had been spending time in the Tyrol—the alps of Northern Italy. She had heart issues. As the climate of Southern California was an alternate destination for those with health concerns, it was decided that Caroline should relocate and live with her daughter. Count Landi would eventually join them.

STARS SHINE IN OAKLAND

December 1931. Elissa and Frances Dee attend the Oakland premier of *The False Madonna*

On November 11, Elissa and her mother boarded the *Mauritania*. Traveling companions included actor Leslie Howard, who would later team with Elissa in a radio broadcast of *Monsieur Beaucaire*. As Landi wasn't due back at Fox for another month, she and Caroline took time settling into her home in Pacific Palisades, with the help of two servants and a cook. Also on hand was a teenager who, several months back, had hitchhiked from Texas to Hollywood where he asked Elissa for a meal—she hired him on the spot as her gardener.[106]

Naturally, the press revived interest in Caroline's royal roots, to which Elissa reluctantly offered, "I have always taken the story for granted. The tale of my ancestry is like a novel, dramatic, fantastic ... ."[107] Some took her statements as a denial of her mother's claims. London critic Cedric Belfrage quipped, "Elissa Landi is now reported to be busy denying that she denied that she's all filled up with blue blood."[108] *Modern Screen* contracted with Catherine Radziwill, a Lithuanian aristocrat who was involved in several scandals herself, to write the article "Refutation," debunking the idea of Caroline's connection to the House of Hapsburg. When asked why Radziwill would refute Caroline's claims, Elissa replied, "Perhaps she needed the money."[109]

Elissa was invited to Oakland, California for the grand opening of the city's $3 Million Paramount Theatre. On the evening of December 16, she was joined by California Governor James Rolph, Irene Dunne, Frances Dee, John Boles, and Landi's good friend Marguerite Churchill. A crowd of 10,000 people were on hand, 3,500 of whom filled the theater to capacity. *The False Madonna* was the feature presentation, starring Kay Francis, also in attendance. Prior to the screening of this improbable mother-son yarn, stars took turns going on stage. *San Francisco Chronicle* noted, "The lovely Elissa Landi said a few words and proved to be charming and gracious."

Back in Hollywood, Caroline was receiving raves for her pastries—echoes of her old confectionary shop in Vancouver. Louella Parsons enthused, "I have just eaten Countess Landi's crepe suzette. They melt in your mouth; they also do terrible things to your figure. But I simply had to meet Elissa's mother after the reports given me of her charm, to say nothing of her culinary ability." Weeks later, Parsons hailed Elissa as having one of the screen's finest minds. "There isn't any subject that she cannot discuss understandingly," said Parsons. "Everyone looked with interest last week when she was lunching with Stanley Baldwin, well-known Socialist. They were so engrossed in conversation that neither seemed to see anyone else. It wasn't a flirtatious interest, either. Elissa was merely seeking to know more about the subject of socialism that is now upsetting the world."[110] Baldwin, a former (and future) Prime Minister, was a part of the Conservative Party's left-wing. He championed workers and gave his own employees an eight-hour-day long before the question excited the House of Commons. Baldwin cautioned fellow Conservatives, "If we are to live as a party we must live for the people in the widest sense. Every future Government must be Socialistic." Baldwin was also influential in getting women the right to vote at age 21 (1928).

<<>>

Devil's Lottery (1932) with Alexander Kirkland (Fox)

In January 1932, Landi completed *Devil's Lottery*. Director Sam Taylor suggested she help amplify the soundtrack by joining (off-screen) the mutterings and yelling in crowd scenes. Elissa enjoyed herself. The story's slender thread dealt with Calcutta sweepstake winners whose lives are drastically changed by cold, hard cash. There is a society beauty of questionable reputation (Landi) and her blackmailing lover (Paul Cavanagh), a young American student (Alexander Kirkland), a disabled war veteran (Ralph Morgan), a nagging, English cockney (Beryl Mercer) and her gambling, prize-fighter son (Victor McLaglen).

In 1974, film historian William K. Everson introduced a revival of *Devil's Lottery* indicating that it was "too good a programmer to remain totally buried. It reminds us what a warm personality Elissa Landi could be. Her performances had vitality, subtlety and sometimes real passion. But the big treat of *Devil's Lottery* will be the treatment meted out to Beryl Mercer."[111] On screen, Mercer ends up suffocating in a clothes closet! Director Taylor asked Elissa to offer a blood-curdling scream off-camera (in lieu of the actress playing the maid) when Mercer's body is discovered. *Devil's Lottery* has its merits. The candid, pre-Code flavor allowed the lead characters to evolve into more genuine versions of themselves.

Motion Picture Herald admired Landi's ability to tackle a "tough part" and "make more out of it than was possible." *Bioscope* observed, "Landi fills to the letter the role of the haughty society beauty." The reviewer felt that the final scenes "fell flat." While audiences expected Landi and Kirkland to run off to the Riviera, the final match of Landi and the crippled Ralph Morgan makes more sense. Landi was deft in her ability to underscore the humanity her character had realized. While Elissa's gracious, natural presence enhanced the proceedings, *Devil's Lottery* lost Fox $128,000.

The Woman in Room 13 was released in May. Landi portrayed a composer whose new father-in-law hires her ex-husband detective (Ralph Bellamy) to spy on her suspected infidelity. Bellamy determines to put Landi's *new* husband (Neil Hamilton) behind bars. Also in the mix is Landi's client (Gilbert Roland) who ends up being murdered by one of his kept women (Myrna Loy). Landi falls into Bellamy's trap, implicating herself by chatting into a Dictaphone! One critic mused, "The general feeling is that everyone talks too much and that there would have been no complications had this been a silent movie. One sometimes wishes Landi would write a story for herself."[112] "It might just as well never been filmed at all," moaned *Modern*

Screen. (It was reported that Landi's own piano composition was used as incidental music).[113]

The Woman in Room 13 (1932) with Neil Hamilton (Fox)

In 1980, Lawrence J. Quirk commented on Myrna Loy's "small and thankless" supporting role. "Practically nothing good could be said about *The Woman in Room 13*, a highly forgettable film. Landi was in her element as a star in 1932, but her talents were wasted in this foolishness."[114] Occasionally, Elissa and Myrna were seen along the Beverly Hills bridle path, enjoying each other's company. Loy recalled in her 1987 autobiography *Being and Becoming*,

> I remember menacing Elissa Landi in a couple of her starring vehicles; she was lean and bright, with wonderful humor, and we became friends to a certain extent. She asked me to some of her cocktail parties, where she always had worldly, interesting people, whose conversation ranged way beyond the picture business.[115]

Co-star Neil Hamilton reflected on his many leading ladies and rated Elissa "the wittiest." "She says things and then looks at you for a comeback. I stand there and guffaw and wish I could crawl into a knothole."[116] At this point in Landi's career, a sense of humor was essential.

<<>>

Elissa and her black mare

While Landi was filming *Woman in Room 13*, her third book was released. Fresh from horseback riding, and lounging around home in green pajamas, she offered an interview to Katherine Albert. Albert observed, "I felt immediately the strange vitality of the woman. Since writing was first with her, it is that she loves more than acting. She spoke dramatically of the glory of living in a secret world, of one's own creating." Landi's latest secret world, *House for Sale*, dealt with a woman's right to a career. The protagonist Elsa symbolized the tragic consequences of a woman who abandons a promising career so that her egotistical husband might be successful. Ohio critic W. Ward Marsh summed up,

House for Sale is rather a curious novel. Her heroine is a woman past middle age. Her husband is dead. Her children are grown. The house, which has known perhaps more heartaches than joys has been sold. Everything must go. The woman relives her life. Some of it is vital, stirring and poignant ... but for the most part it is dull going.[117]

American Mercury noted, "There is not much plot. Miss Landi is concerned always with the psychological reactions of her characters and she describes them with considerable skill." Elissa was triggered to write the story when her mother was in the process of moving. When no one showed interest in an old mahogany table, Elissa began to recall all the family decisions that were made around that table. "If it means that much to me," she thought, "how much more it must mean to her."[118] *House for Sale* used a lot of American slang. "American slang," enthused Landi, "is the most interesting slang in the world. The French are adopting American slang and so are the English." She had even felt its impact when riding a horse.

I went riding on a black, snorting little mare the other day. Her mouth was so soft that you couldn't guide her by the bridle and she wouldn't stop running. I said "Whoa!" in various tones of voice, but she paid no attention. At last I shouted: "Whoa, you great big stiff!" and she stopped instantly.[119]

Elissa enjoyed studying the origins of slang. "I hope to qualify as an expert in slang research someday," she indicated. "My favorite American slang expression right now is 'haywire'." One fan who went "haywire" for *House for Sale* was Joan Crawford. Photographer Cecil Beaton observed Crawford devouring everything Landi had written. "Miss Crawford," he recalled, "became obsessed with the great, lady-like quality of Elissa Landi." Crawford, according to Beaton, was dealing with an inferiority complex.[120]

<<>>

Melvyn Douglas was set to co-star in Landi's next film, *Burnt Offerings*—set in Africa. Much of the location shooting took place on Catalina Island. While early portions were being filmed, Douglas dropped out. His recent release, *Prestige* (1932), with Ann Harding, had similar themes set in Indochina, and a script which touted the superiority of the white race. Harding was horrified when she saw the final print and begged RKO to allow her to buy and destroy the negative. No doubt Douglas (who would later co-star with Landi on stage) didn't want a repeat of *Prestige*. He was replaced by Paul Lukas. *Burnt Offerings* became *Undesirable Woman*, then finally *Passport to Hell*.

Passport to Hell **(1932) with Warner Oland (Fox)**

The film picked up where *The Yellow Ticket* left off, at the outset of WWI. Landi, an Englishwoman with a scandalous past, is deemed an "undesirable" presence in the British colony of Accra. When questioned by authorities about her reputation, she complacently replies, "Quite a lot to live down, isn't it?" She is deported to German-occupied Cameroon. Landi declares their decision "a passport to Hell!" Sure enough, she heads straight ... in that direction. Upon her arrival in Cameroon, England declares war on Germany. Landi is taken into custody. A smitten young German officer (Alexander Kirkland) proposes marriage. She accepts, much to the horror of his father (Warner Oland), the Commander of Military Police. Landi is pleased that she has "tricked the uniform"—a taste of retribution for all the grief she has suffered from military brass.

Passport to Hell (1932) with Paul Lukas (Fox)

The inevitable love triangle erupts when Kirkland relocates to an interior jungle post. Government engineer Paul Lukas shows up, and Landi offers to sharpen not only his pencils, but his libido. "I'm in love for the first time in my life!" she swoons. Soon after her declaration, *Passport to Hell* erupts into a mix of treason, suicide and another deportation (to Manila) for Landi. We have witnessed her tough edges soften with warmth, nuance and sensitivity. She comes across as genuine, although, as *Film Daily* points out, Landi was "handicapped" by an obvious story and "hackneyed" dialogue. Racial stereotyping of native peoples was another drawback —"they're all thieves," Kirkland cautions Landi.

Motion Picture observed, "Elissa Landi's distinction and intelligent beauty dignify a rather routine part into an authentic characterization." A small town theater manager in Minnesota commented to *Motion Picture Herald*, "The best Landi picture to date. Why don't they give Landi some better stories? She is a great actress, better than some others that are supposed to be big shots." Despite the tepid critical and box-office response, Fox attempted to reissue *Passport to Hell* a few years later. The Hays Office refused, indicating that Landi's adulterous interlude with Lukas lacked "the proper compensating moral values." *Passport to Hell* lost Fox $172,000.

Passport to Hell (1932) "Quite a lot to live down, isn't it?" (Fox)

<<>>

Before completing her seventh film for Fox, Landi already knew the score. Two years later, she summed up, "It is hard to work for a studio when you know it is antagonistic toward you from the start. I discovered that I hadn't been wanted at all; that it only bid for my services to spite the others. I saw myself trampled beneath a procession of impossible heroines."[121] Film/theater critic Elinor Hughes had suspected that Landi was "out of luck, through no fault of her own, but simply through criminal mismanagement."

"Thick-skulled" Winfield Sheehan, receives Best Picture Oscar for
***Cavalcade* (1933)**

Elissa used the metaphor of "a large bottle with a very narrow neck" in describing Fox Studio. "This bottle," she explained, "contains many fine things—ideas, talent, settings, actors ... until it has been painstakingly filtered through the narrow neck, the thick skull of the little man in the main office.

Call him what you please, supervisor, chief."[122] William Fox, who had lost control over his film empire in 1930, couldn't be blamed. Most likely the "thick skull" Elissa referred to was production head, Winfield Sheehan— the man who had hired her. Gossip columnist Louella Parsons blabbed that Sheehan had told Elissa that her emotions "were too mental." In an obvious put-down to Landi's writing career, he advised, "Stop being literary. Act your roles as if you mean them." Parsons had the audacity to claim that Landi "took his advice to heart."[123] Former Fox player Jeanette MacDonald had had her problems with Sheehan. She confided in a letter to her lover and business manager Robert Richie, "When I count the doors I have to go through to see Mr. Sheehan, I bet that when I die, if I've been good, I won't have to pass as many doors to get to see God."[124] MacDonald promptly left the studio in 1931, following a three-picture contract.

The Fox empire, under the scrutiny of a bank-mandated reorganization, had reason to give Landi a well-deserved break from playing "impossible heroines." For several months a quiet gent named Don McIntyre was on the lot in charge of moving physical properties between locations. Stars, crew-members and executives treated him as a nuisance. The shock came when it was revealed that he was a secret agent for Chase National Bank—an institution that had loaned millions to Fox. McIntyre was actually an efficiency expert. The *only* individual who had treated him with respect was Elissa Landi, who enjoyed engaging him in conversation.

On one occasion McIntyre commented to Elissa, "It seems as if there is a great deal of waste around here." Landi had been waiting over an hour for costumes to arrive. She had telephoned, sent messages via errand boys ... nothing. "I'll see what temperament will do!" she told him, picking up the phone one more time. McIntyre listened as Elissa went on a tirade. Five minutes later the costumes showed up. McIntyre made a note of it. When the truth of his identity was finally revealed, Landi told him, "I suppose now that you're God around here I'll have to call you 'Mr.'" McIntyre smiled, "No. I'm only God's office boy."[125] Walter Winchell went so far as to refer to McIntyre as "Elissa Landi's new sugar-pie." Landi's reward ... a well-deserved loan-out that enabled her to ascend, momentarily, into the Hollywood firmament under the guidance of the reputable Cecil B. DeMille.

It was Landi's eyes that inspired DeMille to cast her as the Christian girl in *The Sign of the Cross*, a major hit for the veteran director. "She has the spirit and depth of the ages in her eyes," DeMille declared. In truth, Elissa had been diagnosed with "arthritis of the eye nerves" from overexposure to studio Klieg lights. Prior to her first loan-out from Fox, she was awarded a "vacation" in the hospital so "the spirit and depth of the ages" could take a brief respite, before being fed to the lions.

The Sign of the Cross (1932) Cecil B. DeMille directs Fredric March and Landi. Karl Struss (photographer) (Paramount)

Landi directs DeMille

Chapter 7
DeMille & Divorce

Landi's loan-out to Paramount for Cecil B. DeMille's *The Sign of the Cross* offered visibility and pushed her career forward. Shot between July–September 1932, *Sign of the Cross* created a sensation, making a profit of over $600,000. It also generated much controversy. DeMille's epic mix of Roman lust and Christian persecution, helped prompt the Catholic Church to establish The Legion of Decency. At a June 1934 Cleveland rally, Bishop Joseph Schrembs addressed 50,000 from the pulpit, demanding, "Purify Hollywood, or destroy Hollywood! The only language that these dealers in smut understand is the language of the tinkling cash register. Empty their tills ... ."[126] The new Production Code went into effect the following month. It's repercussions would be felt for decades.

After DeMille had tested such popular stars as Ann Harding, Loretta Young, and Sylvia Sidney, Elissa was awarded the role of Mercia, an innocent Christian girl. DeMille declared, "I am convinced that she is endowed with the rare quality of etherealism more than any girl in Hollywood."[127] Fredric March was cast in the male lead as Marcus Superbus, a high-ranking Roman official. As filming began, writer Elsie Janis visited the set at 1a.m. for an all-night shoot. Janis observed a scene in which arrows targeted Mercia's father. There were numerous takes. "I watched Elissa find her white-bearded old father shot to death about seven times. Never a sign of fatigue or resentment on her part. Due to arrow trouble, beard slipping, fake blood not flowing freely enough, they were still killing the distinguished old Christian when I had to leave or send for my sleeping bag."[128]

Janis noted that *between* takes Landi was more like Peter Pan than the "ethereal" Mercia. "She has a decided boyish quality which would manifest itself immediately after a scene. She would stride from the range of the camera, kidding the property man, tossing a line to an extra, or landing a slap on the back of Fredric March." Quite possibly Elissa's slap may have been a form of retribution. March was notorious for putting his hands where they weren't welcome. Claudette Colbert, as the seductive Empress Poppaea, complained years afterward, "Freddie March was the worst womanizer I ever knew. His hands had twenty fingers, I swear, and they were always on my ass."[129]

Sign of the Cross (based on a creaky 1895 play) was dazzling to look at and filled with the excesses for which Cecil B. DeMille was known. Charles Laughton (in his American film debut) as Emperor Nero sat on the throne next to his scantily clad male concubine. As the effete pagan ruler who languishes in self-abandonment, Laughton stole the show. DeMille went so far as to include a sensuous lesbian interlude, "The Naked Moon," in which dancer Joyzelle Joyner attempts to seduce the angelic Landi during an orgy. (*Harrison Reports* deduced, "The average adult will not understand that it is a Lesbian dance and hardly any of the adolescents will know what is happening.") Years later, DeMille's granddaughter Cecilia recalled that Will Hays, head of the Production Code, had asked DeMille prior to the film's release what he was going to do about the "Lesbian Dance." DeMille replied, "Not a damn thing."[130]

Roman persecution of Christians evolves into "The Greatest Show on Earth," with stampeding elephants, crocodiles, battling pygmies and Christian-hungry lions. Landi's Mercia, refusing to renounce her faith in exchange for freedom, was last to enter the blood-fest arena. She is joined by March, who succumbs to his own passion for Mercia rather than the holy cross. A savvy Houston critic observed that March's "ultimate sacrifice suggests something more fleshy than spiritual." Even so, DeMille deemed it inappropriate for the duo to lock lips on screen.

Elissa resists the charms of Joyzelle (Paramount)

Laughton and paramour George Bruggeman (Paramount)

Motion Picture Herald predicted that audiences "will shudder, they will gasp, they will cry, and they will love it, provided their sensibilities survive the odors of Lesbos and de Sade. Miss Landi's picture roles have not always been so fortunate, but here she displays real dramatic power and beauty." *Boston Herald* enthused, "Elissa Landi in her right métier at last, plays Mercia with such simplicity and beauty—that innocence and virtue fairly come into their own. Charles Laughton creates a gem of a characterization as Nero—soft, effeminate, cruel and vicious. It is only to be regretted that there is so little of him on the screen." When Laughton returned to England he admitted, "Elissa Landi, the leading lady, I never met at all." In London, critic James Agate mused, "As Nero Mr. Charles Laughton enjoys himself hugely, playing that emperor as the flaunting extravagant quean [sic] he probably was."[131] Journalist Sydney Tremayne singled out Landi for praise, "The outstanding performance among all this grandiose and spectacular falsity is that of Elissa Landi ... in an extremely difficult part she manages to skirt the obvious pits of sentimentality and religiosity."[132]

When reissued in 1938 and 1944, censors removed the controversial excesses from the negative of *Sign of the Cross*. Fortunately, DeMille kept a complete print of the film. In 1989, UCLA restored the film to its original content. Elissa apparently was pleased with DeMille and vice-versa. "While working with Cecil B. DeMille," she said, "he told me that there was one picture he would really like to make with me, and it was *Joan of Arc*."[133] This had been a dream-role of Elissa's since her youth. Unfortunately, Landi and DeMille would only reteam on radio.

<<>>

While she was filming *Sign of the Cross*, John Lawrence paid his wife a visit. Elissa hoped he would make Hollywood a permanent stay, and obtained a job for him. He declined the offer. Prior to his arrival in August, Elissa opened up to the reputable Gladys Hall, founding member of the Hollywood Women's Press Club.

I believe that women need to plan their lives. I speak from personal experience ... I have planned mine. First of all, I want children. They are to me the most important thing in all of life. I plan to live here, in Hollywood, where I have bought my home. My mother is with me and my husband arrives day after tomorrow. In a year or two I plan to have my first child.[134]

On the DeMille set. Lots to contemplate.

Instead of making plans for a family, John Lawrence spent time describing his love affairs to Elissa and encouraged her to "seek similar diversion."[135] The Wild West party that Elissa and John hosted on September 17, ended up being a final bow to their relationship. Elissa's drawing room was transformed into a saloon. Pictures of race horses, prize-fighters and burlesque queens covered the walls. Following this hoe-down, the couple opted to separate. On September 23, 1932, Lawrence flew to New York, bound for London. He quipped to reporters, "I'm quite in love with Hollywood, but there are people in London who will spend the winter in jail if I don't go back." Even so, Landi continued to forward Lawrence $100 a month, hoping for a reconciliation. Elissa had commented to Gladys Hall, "The day will come when we will want companionship and someone to talk over the journey with—and children grown up about us and starting the great adventure afresh." Soon after John's departure, Elissa went to Vancouver. Authorities had refused to extend her visitor's permit. She hoped to be assigned a quota number, in order to return to the U.S. as an immigrant.

<<>>

Landi co-stars with Ronald Colman in *The Masquerader* (1933) (UA)

Upon her return to Hollywood, Landi had the good fortune to be teamed with Ronald Colman in Samuel Goldwyn's *The Masquerader*. The co-stars enjoyed a mutual sense of humor. Colman struggled with the line: "The car's in the drive and your coat's in the car." When he finally got the right tempo, he couldn't resist adding, "God's in his heaven, all's right with the world!" From across the sound stage Elissa's voice rang out, "With a hey-nonny-nonny and a hot-cha-cha!"[136] (The troublesome line was eliminated from the final print). Frivolity subsided while Landi dealt with a serious case of influenza. Production was held up for weeks. Goldwyn went so far as to test Diana Wynyard for the role, just in case. Landi was more optimistic. While recuperating, she composed the lilting *Sonata in F Minor* for the piano—which she plays on screen.

In a dual role, Colman portrays Sir John Chilchote, a member of Parliament, and his look-alike cousin John Loder, a political journalist. Chilchote persuades the cousin to fill-in for him professionally, while he deals with drug and alcohol addiction. Censors were aghast when the script also allowed the cousin to fill in ... domestically. Chilchote's neglected wife Eve (Landi) hasn't a clue. For good measure, Chilchote's mistress (Juliette Compton) suspects something's amiss. Suspense builds during the budding romance of Loder and Eve. By the time Chilchote dies from an overdose, Eve is aware of the masquerade and embraces marital bliss with her imposter husband. Pre-Code flavor remains intact for the technically adulterous duo. *The Masquerader* has the uncanny ability to beguile. Excellent performances, including Halliwell Hobbes' brilliant take as Chilchote's faithful man-servant, were complemented by the deep-focus camerawork of Gregg Toland, and director Richard Wallace's ability to make the fantastic seem plausible.

D.C.'s *Evening Star* praised Colman and Landi, saying "Their work throughout ... is of the kind that inspires applause." *Film Daily* nodded, "Colman gives an arresting dual performance ... Elissa Landi plays the wife beautifully." *Hollywood Filmograph* concluded, "Elissa Landi has at last been given something worthy of her talents and it is unfortunate that the studio to whom she is under contract does not realize the value of this fine player."

The Masquerader was among the box-office champs for 1933. Although there were previews in February, release was held until August, as it would be Colman's only film in1933. He and Goldwyn, after numerous films together, parted ways. Goldwyn's publicity chief informed columnist Sidney Skolsky that Colman often took a nip of liquor prior to making love on screen. Skolsky told readers that Colman "feels that he looks better for pictures when moderately dissipated."[137] The actor sued Goldwyn, asking for $2 million in damages. In the aftermath, Colman dropped his libel suit and opted for an extended vacation from Hollywood.

The Masquerader is to be counted among Elissa Landi's best. Although the focus was on Colman's admirable dual challenge, Landi's unique persona and natural nuance was rarely seen to better advantage. Colman himself would successfully take on another double role in the popular, if less plausible epic, *The Prisoner of Zenda* (1937).

‹‹››

Autumn 1932. Elissa drove her roadster across the Mojave Desert to Yosemite National Park—a 300 mile trip. At the historic Ahwahnee Hotel she enjoyed the blaze of fall colors, while working on the last chapters of her fourth novel, *The Ancestor*. In January, Elissa sojourned to Calexico, Mexico, to await a quota number from Italy so she could obtain a new visa. Her previous trip to Vancouver was jinxed by Labor Department regulations. Passport troubles affected 300 Hollywood players, who faced deportation. Squads of federal agents investigated claims that some film colony foreign residents were using falsified passports. An Ohio editor blasted the investigation as treating actors as if they were public enemies. "It might bring great harm to the motion picture industry ... an unfortunate and short sighted piece of red-tape of a zealous immigration department." Elissa solved her dilemma, for the time being, by filing naturalization papers. Being the wife of an English barrister complicated things.

Prior to her departure to Mexico, Landi attended the premier of Noel Coward's acclaimed *Cavalcade*. She was accompanied by Alexander Kirkland for the opening at Grauman's Chinese Theater. Movietone news captured the attractive pair as they smiled for the camera. Kirkland took Landi's arm for a photogenic jaunt to the left, remarking, "Elissa, I hope Frank Lloyd has one of the swell-est pictures in the world." Landi chimes in, "So do I!" Their wish was granted. Lloyd received an Academy Award for Best Director, and Fox studio won its first Academy Award for Best Picture.

Kirkland was the model for a character named Tony in the 1933 gay romance novel *Better Angel*. It was written by his friend Forman Brown (under the pen name Richard Meeker). The positive slant on gay relationships was unusual for the time. Brown waited until 1995 before revealing the facts behind the fiction.[138] In 1945, Landi and Kirkland would reteam on stage in Noel Coward's *Blithe Spirit*.

Alexander Kirkland escorts Elissa to the premier of *Cavalcade* (1933) at Grauman's Chinese Theater

<<>>

Back at Fox, Landi was offered the lead in *The Warrior's Husband*. A recent Broadway revival of the play had landed Katharine Hepburn a RKO contract. In this romantic satire of Greek mythology, set in the Amazon, males were the weaker sex. Fox publicized "real-life drag artists had been hired to portray the 'men'."[139] Landi portrayed Antiope, a swaggering commander of the female armed forces. When confronted with the strapping masculinity of Theseus, a Greek warrior (David Manners), Antiope wields her sword. Theseus wields a passionate kiss, winning the battle.

The Warrior's Husband (1933) with David Manners (Fox)

Director Walter Lang offered pre-Code flourishes to this gender-bender, as when Amazon women salute their beloved queen Hippolyta (Marjorie Rambeau) with a raised middle finger. Critics gave a thumbs up to *The Warrior's Husband*, although *Harrison Reports* cautioned that the film was "not suitable ... for Sundays." *Variety* rated Landi's performance her "best screen work to date." Critic for the *Oregonian* raved, "Elissa Landi breaks through with an entirely different characterization. Her performance is the artistic highlight of the production." *Boston Herald* echoed, "It serves to supply Landi with her best screen role; breezy, charming and natural."

Although Hepburn made a screen test for the lead with John Ford, Fox decided on Landi, who admitted, "I had to fight to get them to let me do it."[140] She enjoyed playing Antiope, and would revive it on stage in 1938. Was Hepburn miffed with Landi's success? Possibly. Journalist Max Breen told about Landi and Hepburn meeting at a dinner party at Jesse Lasky's home, where the producer first screened *The Warrior's Husband*.

> Elissa, being the diplomat, deferentially consulted the star as to which scene in the film she liked best. "Oh," replied Katie promptly, "the scene I like is the one where you run across the field and vault a fence; it seemed to me to have so much more life and spirit than the other scenes."[141]

The scene, of course, had been played by Landi's double. Hepburn's escort, Doug Fairbanks Jr., and other guests were momentarily dumbstruck at Kate's tactless remark. Elissa needn't have been offended. As Breen points out, it was the "kind of brick that Katie ... habitually dropped." Fairbanks himself later confessed that Hepburn left him "romantically tongue-tied."[142]

Amazon warrior Landi (Fox)

The Warrior's Husband was screened in 2019 at the Metropolitan Museum of Art. I asked publisher Andrew Wentink what he thought of the film and Landi's take on the role. Wentink responded,

> One can see from Elissa Landi's performance how much influence the brashness of early Hepburn had on the characterization. Nevertheless, Landi makes Antiope her own to reveal a dynamic component of her talent that few of her other film roles offered her. As for the film, it is absolutely bold and outrageous in its concept. It plays havoc with gender stereotypes that would be audacious even today. The cast is excellent across the board. The production values are extremely impressive. It definitely should be brought into the canon, so to speak, of pre-Code classics.[143]

The Warrior's Husband entertains with an intentional routine of slapstick and parody of gender roles. As Wentink points out, the film offered a rare glimpse of Landi's persona that few of her screen roles offered. She intrigues. She impresses. She holds your attention.

<<>>

Elissa's final film for Fox, *I Loved You Wednesday,* had flopped on Broadway. The film also failed to congeal into anything that resembled reality. In Paris, a youthful prima ballerina (Landi) is involved with a philandering American architect (Victor Jory) who, after six months, reveals that he has a wife. Landi heads to South America where she falls for a construction engineer (Warner Baxter). Landi returns to Paris to flutter upon the stage in the strange concoction "Dance of the Maidens"—amongst scantily-clad mythical male warriors who appear to be after one maiden's ... stuffed pussycat. Elissa, svelte and graceful, had the opportunity to be alongside George Bruggeman, who had been awarded "The Most Perfectly Developed Male Body of 1928."

I Loved You Wednesday (1933) with Warner Baxter (Fox)

I Loved You Wednesday - George Bruggeman pulls Landi away from June Lang (Fox)

Baxter heads to Boulder, Colorado, where we witness endless footage of crews building the Hoover Dam. Gratuitous explosions suddenly push the narrative five years forward. Landi and Baxter reunite in New York, where ex-lover Jory also pops up. As the trio heads toward a speakeasy, Baxter gives a nod to Jory and suggests to Landi, "We might adopt him!" It might have helped if they had—a romantic *menage a trois* with pre-Code punch. Instead, we are obligated to watch Landi attempt to run off with Jory until she recalls something his wife had told her, "He's incapable of loving anyone." A fade-out Baxter-Landi kiss designates a happy, if unconvincing, ending. The script failed to make sense of any of these relationships.

Landi was at her liveliest (and loveliest) in *I Loved You Wednesday*, but as *Film Daily* assessed, "Neither Warner Baxter nor Elissa Landi has a role offering much opportunity." Another critic moaned that the cast "seemed more like robots than individuals." Landi wails, "Why does it have to end so shabbily?"—a line that aptly described *I Loved You Wednesday*, as well as her career at Fox, where she felt stuck playing women of questionable character. Landi refused to do retakes for the film, and backed out of doing her next assignment *I Am a Widow*. On July 7, 1933, her contract with Fox was "dissolved by mutual consent."

<<>>

Helping to assuage Elissa's break from Fox was her houseguest, New York composer/pianist Abram Chasins. The two had met in 1931, after she wrote him a fan letter. During his stay with Elissa in the summer of 1933, she wrote lyrics to Chasins' composition *Offering of Eros*. She also bought Chasins a new Packard. When she filed for divorce the following year (May 16, 1934), she claimed that during Chasins' visit, husband Lawrence "repudiated me."[144] Lawrence's renunciation is puzzling, as he had suggested an open relationship two years prior. Nonetheless, John Lawrence countersued for divorce in December 1934, accusing Elissa of "misconduct," naming Chasins as co-respondent. By that time, a fan magazine fabricated a tale saying that the Landi-Chasins relationship was "Hollywood's Most Beautiful Friendship."

Composer Abram Chasins

Some have suggested that Elissa and Katharine Hepburn were briefly involved in an intimate friendship. When Elissa accompanied her mother to New York in November 1933, they were photographed with Hepburn at Burbank Airport— the two stars swathed in matching fur coats. Once aboard, the trio sat together. Caroline had decided to spend time with her husband who was in Italy. Hepburn, estranged from her own husband, was set to start rehearsals for a tryout of *The Lake*, which opened on Broadway that December. Landi, manuscript in hand, was set to meet with her publisher (Doubleday) regarding her latest book, *The Ancestor*. There was also talk of Landi returning to Broadway in a production of the Hungarian play, *Angel*. Louella Parsons revealed that Landi and Hepburn "became great friends during their sky journey and after they reached New York they saw each other on several occasions."

November 1933. Elissa, Caroline, and Hepburn at the Burbank Airport

In Hepburn's 1991 autobiography *Me*, she recalled meeting producer Al Woods in 1930. She asked him who had the female lead in *A Farewell to Arms*, a role she hoped to try out for. "He said Elissa Landi," wrote Hepburn. "That's all there was to it."[145] And, that's all Hepburn had to say about Landi. In 2007, Hepburn biographer William J. Mann indicated, "there is no evidence, aside from a few photographs, of an affair." Mann contacted Landi's daughter Caroline Thomas. Caroline told Mann that she had "heard the stories ... but had no way of knowing if they were true."[146]

No doubt Landi wouldn't have paid much attention to such rumors. She was comfortable in her own skin, as witnessed by Elsie Janis. Elissa showed up at Janis' home one afternoon, stepped outside, eyed the swimming pool, and asked her host, "May I go in without a top?" Janis, amused by the request, answered, "You may go in any way you like."[147]

< >

Now freelancing, Landi signed for two features: *By Candlelight* (Universal), and *Man of Two Worlds* (RKO). Director James Whale, fresh from success with *The Invisible Man*, lent his talent to the breezy scenario of *By Candlelight*, in which a lovelorn butler (Paul Lukas) impersonates his employer, a nobleman (Nils Asther), in an attempt to impress Marie (Landi), a woman he assumes to be of royal blood. Fact was, Marie is concealing her own identity: a maid. Asther finds the situation amusing, and boosts Lukas' seduction by pretending to be *his* butler. As characters mirror each other, the pretense and sham of nobility comes to the fore. Landi's native intelligence and piercing eyes demand attention, and she did full justice to her role. Nils Asther generated the perfect wit and nuance to compliment Whale's brisk pace. Paul Lukas, unfortunately, was miscast. His edgy overreactions stifled a role that better suited the amused charm of a Herbert Marshall.

By Candlelight (1933) directed by James Whale (Universal)

London's *The Sketch* enthused, "*By Candlelight* gives James Whale an opportunity to prove that he possesses a light directorial touch far removed from his handling of the Frankenstein school. He lends fluency to a piquant story of amorous cross-purposes." New York's *Daily Mirror* found Elissa "bewitching." In 2009, prior to a screening of *By Candlelight* in New York, writer/critic David Noh detailed, "Whale brings his formidable, omniscient sophistication and gay-man's laser-like attention to ... glamour and sensuality. From Vienna to Monte Carlo the sexy ruse plays itself out in various luxurious hotel rooms and casinos, until the truth comes out. The comic pacing is impeccable. Nils Asther plays with unparalleled grace and *savoir-faire*. Elissa Landi has her best screen role. She makes Marie an entrancing creature of impulse."[148] Landi had the tempo and simpatico for light comedy, a genre in which she rarely partook. She offered a spirited tipsy scene after Lukas fills her up with cognac, that has its own charm.

Certainly the presence of James Whale lifted Elissa's spirits. It had been almost a decade since the two worked together in the cheeky comedy *Dandy Dick*. During a stopover in Cleveland, en route to New York with her mother, Landi told critic W. Ward Marsh, "I have no idea how fans will take me in *By Candlelight*. There are moments in the picture when I think I clown as much as Chaplin." The film did well at the box-office. Whale noted *By Candlelight* as one of his personal favorites.

Man of Two Worlds was released in March 1934. Audiences didn't buy the over-long tale of an Eskimo named Iago (Francis Lederer) who attempts to mix into British society. As the Arctic hunter with a mystic edge, Iago mistakes the attentions of a lovely socialite (Landi) for love. Ample footage underscores his fascination with her "beautiful white skin." Landi offers Iago a slug of whisky and, bam!— native lust takes hold as he becomes a cliché. "He's nothing but a savage! He tried to make love to me!" she cries. As critic W. Ward Marsh put it, "Our hero suddenly became a villain and the entire illusion was lost, because a lie had been told." Rebuffed, Iago leaves for home. Marsh added, "Miss Landi is cast in a perfectly thankless role. No wonder she cries against Hollywood's handling of her." *Picture Play* countered, "In the most unsympathetic part she has ever played, Miss Landi achieves her best acting."

Man of Two Worlds (1934) with Francis Lederer (RKO)

Landi is emotionally on-cue in a thankless assignment—essentially a supporting role. Lederer does well enough with a difficult task, but gravitates toward wide-eyed exuberance once too often. The film lost RKO $220,000. To director J. Walter Ruben's credit, *Man of Two Worlds* manages to expose the ignorance and deceptions that fuel so-called "civilization." Nonetheless, the film is outdated. RKO's attempt to make the handsome Lederer a matinee idol, as he had been in Czechoslovakia, didn't succeed. Instead of returning to his native people, the talented Lederer became a U.S. citizen and remained active with occasional leads in film, and a successful stage career.

<<>>

Landi, with the help of her friend Elsie Janis, had signed a contract with Columbia Pictures in October 1933. (This was after she refused an offer to sign with MGM.) Elissa was being considered to team with Clark Gable in the production *Night Bus*. While Landi opted to fly to New York with her mother and Hepburn, Claudette Colbert got the role. The film, re-titled

It Happened One Night, won five Academy Awards, including Best Actress. Though Landi lost Gable to Colbert, she was in good spirits and feeling optimistic about her three-year Columbia contract. In mid-January she began her first film for the studio. With a dash of American slang she told one reporter, "Watch my smoke!"[149]

1934 - Landi and the new Fox sensation, Shirley Temple

Chapter 8
"Watch My Smoke!"

The smoke that Landi generated while under contract at Columbia was mostly from cigarettes. After lighting a fresh one during an interview with free-lance writer Malcolm Oettinger, Elissa leaned forward to emphasize her theories on the "thick skulls" that ran Fox. As far as her move to Columbia, helmed by the skull of chief Harry Cohn, Landi offered, "I don't know what he plans for me," and with a sweeping gesture added, "After what I've been through anything will be welcome!"[150] A month later, Cohn agreed to tear up her contract.

Carole Lombard had rejected the showgirl role in Columbia's *Sisters Under the Skin.* She opted to play opposite John Barrymore in the highly successful *Twentieth Century* (in which Landi and Orson Welles would co-star on radio). Landi landed the Lombard role, which left *Vanity Fair* wondering, "Why they ever cast Elissa Landi as a Broadway fly-girl—and let her struggle with 42nd Street slang—is another of those fascinating Hollywood daily mysteries."

Overall, reviews were mixed. *Sisters Under the Skin* centered on the extra-marital affair of a New York millionaire (Frank Morgan) and Blossom Bailey (Landi) the young actress he takes to Paris. Once there, Morgan isn't up to the rigors of romantic passion. After all, he's 49! When Blossom takes fancy to a musician (Joseph Schildkraut), Morgan returns to his wife. So ends what *The New York Sun* described as, "a little ridiculous and sophomoric." Columnist Helen Burns visited the set during filming, and scrutinized Landi's performance. "I couldn't help but feel she was a bit disdainful of Blossom. Another actress might of submerged her own personality into the character, but Elissa never quite forgot that Blossom's ideals were not her ideals, that Blossom's courage was not equal to her own."

When Elissa refused Columbia's request to star opposite Stuart Erwin in *The Party's Over* ... so was her contract. Ann Sothern took her place. *Photoplay* dismissed the film as being in "limbo of anything for a laugh." Elissa explained,

> My relations with Columbia were perfectly agreeable, but their trend is modern, frothy stuff, the sort of thing I can't do. I walked out on *The Party's Over*, because I was to play a second rate stenographer, a sort of stooge to Stuart Erwin. I'm not the type. I couldn't do justice to it or myself.[151]

Sisters Under the Skin (Columbia)

Landi's agents then had the temerity to tie up her salary and bank account. Ad Schulberg-Kenneth Feldman Inc. weren't expecting her to part with Columbia, and sued for $11,000 allegedly due to them.[152] Landi was under the impression that she could be released from her contract, as well as the Schulberg-Feldman theatrical agency, whenever she thought it optimal. She was now left without funds to maintain her home. After recovering from an attack of tonsillitis, Elissa headed to Superior Court. On March 7, 1934, she made a request to remove the attachment. Two weeks later, a judge showed clemency and released some money to her.

During this altercation, Elissa received consolation from her frequent houseguest Abram Chasins, along with opera diva Grace Moore. Moore was pleased with the lyrics that Landi had supplied for Chasins' music, and was preparing to include songs from *Offering to Eros* during an upcoming concert tour. Baritone Nelson Eddy was also adding the songs to his repertoire. A review from *The Pacific Coast Musician* praised "the songs are not at all in the ordinary vein" and "may shock the purist." Landi's lyrics for "If I Were the Rain" reflected,

If I were the rain I would bless you
If I were the sun I would caress you
No trouble or tears would distress you
Ever, ah never ...
If I were the wind I would take you
If I were a kiss I would wake you
And if I were sorrow forsake you
Forever ... forever .... forever ...[153]

Landi herself made a rare public appearance when she took the lead in a choral ensemble presentation of *Song of Solomon* at Hollywood Concert Hall. In May, she entertained in the Screen Actors Guild benefit, joining Ann Harding, Mary Astor and master of ceremonies Eddie Cantor. All this, while filing for divorce.

<<>>

Freelancing once again, Elissa was sought by Universal for the lead in *She*, based on H. Rider Haggard's novel. Edward Laemmle would direct, and Charles Bickford would co-star. In July, they were to start filming at a Rhodesian ranch in South Africa. Copyright issues brought things to a halt.[154] RKO took over the project, and Helen Gahagan got the lead. Landi went to Paramount where she was joined by former co-stars David Manners and Adolphe Menjou in *The Great Flirtation*. Menjou hammed it up as Stephan Karpath, a famous Hungarian actor who is obsessed with the struggling young actress Zita Marishka (Landi). He throws a constant stream of insults, saying she has no talent. Karpath wants Marishka to abandon her career and marry him. She complies aboard ship as they sail to New York. Landi and Menjou effectively utilize Hungarian accents, but Menjou's unrelenting declamations become tiresome.

The Great Flirtation (1934) with David Manners and Adolphe Menjou
(Paramount)

During rehearsals for a new play, Marishka falls in love with playwright Larry Kenyon (David Manners). They engage in an evening of lip-locking by the fire in Kenyon's studio. Manners' warm, natural presence arrives just in time to keep the improbable scenario afloat. Karpath nobly steps aside, an ending that brought more relief than the intended poignancy. *Time* magazine accurately indicated that the film wobbled between comedy and sentiment. *Variety* called it "an endurance contest." One critic groaned, "We are sick of seeing Miss Landi draw second-rate parts in third-rate pictures." Even so, Elissa offered humor and heart to the capricious Marishka. *Boston Herald* noted "Landi has never looked more charming nor played with such flourish and gaiety. What she needs now is the perfect director." Unfortunately, lackluster direction (Ralph Murphy) along with Menjou's overbearing characterization placed unnecessary weight on the film.

The Great Flirtation was released a month before the new Production Code went into effect. The film itself offered no punishment to Landi, a married woman, having an overnight fling with Manners. Off-screen, Elissa offered her own opinions on the subject to the *San Francisco Chronicle*.

> It's absurd. For years we were forced to make pictures for the 12-year-old mind. Now our pictures are for 12-year-old people ... and as a result every subtle nuance ... everything that might be beautiful or poignant in a picture is yanked out. In England two sets of pictures are made. One for children and childish adults. The other for adults with adult minds. That's the only intelligent kind of censorship. The only balm in the present regime is the hope that this new mania for purity in pictures will wear itself out and censorship will adapt itself to the modern trend.[155]

It would be another 30 years before the grip of the Production Code began to crumble. Being upfront with opinions on censorship was part of Elissa's penchant for what one interviewer recognized as an "aggressively democratic spirit." "This picture business does soften us," Elissa admitted.

"We forget that there is poverty and genuine distress outside … we forget about the rest of the world. We cease to think."[156] When accused of being high-hat, she insisted, "I am *not*. I chew gum insidiously, ride to the studio every day in a nondescript little Ford and halloa [sic] at scene shifters and associate producers along the way."[157] She recognized that a variety of people broadened her viewpoint. Writer Dickson Morley observed of Landi, "Her servants are strikingly loyal and there's a reason"—she afforded her employees the best living conditions. "I want them to be house-proud," she stated, "to have genuine attachment for me and for their home."

<<>>

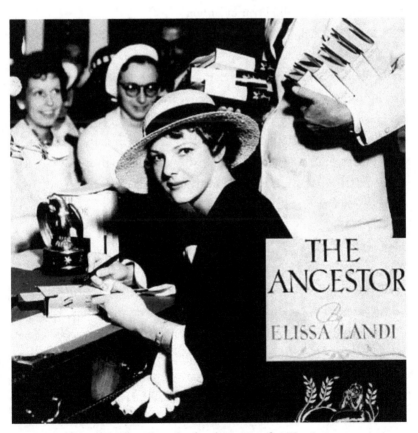

June 1934. Los Angeles book signing for *The Ancestor*

Landi began promoting the release of her fourth novel, *The Ancestor*, which was (surprisingly) dedicated to her almost ex-husband John Lawrence. Prior to publication, Elissa met with her publisher in New York, who spent his time smoothing out transitions and deleting expletives. Elissa's stream of consciousness style dealt with a lyric soprano who abandons cinema to pursue the concert stage. Bent on defying convention, she divides her romantic notions between a fifty-year-old American steel magnate, who promises to marry her if she gets pregnant, and a young unknown British violinist. After a passionate interlude with the violinist, the magnate fulfills his promise. A New Jersey critic praised, "Miss Landi enhances the tale with a remarkable frankness of speech and thought that immediately places her above and beyond the run-of-the-mill type of author."

Elissa's connection to music was woven into her acting, as well as her novels. "Skilled acting is a rhythmic art," she explained, "and only those who are deeply aware of music and rhythm can hope to capture its fullest flexibility. Timing is the very soul of dramatic representation." George Gershwin had recognized early on that music was at the core of her thespian skill .... "a symphony of emotion." Landi also recognized that "the curious syncopation of gesture and speech" extended itself into, what she referred to as, "the business of *living*." "If *your* music is to sound forth as it should," she concluded, "your entire person must be relaxed, easy, free."[158]

The Count of Monte Cristo

Landi had the good fortune to be cast in *The Count of Monte Cristo* opposite Britain's romantic lead Robert Donat. The United Artists film, based on a novel by Alexandre Dumas, would prove to be a huge success. Donat offered an attentive delineation of Edmund Dantes, a French sailor from Marseilles in the early 1800's. Dantes is wrongfully imprisoned on the day of his engagement to sweetheart Mercedes (Landi). Her aristocratic mother was not pleased with her daughter's decision to marry a sailor. Dantes soon discovers the truth behind a scheme that puts him behind bars. After many years, Dantes escapes inside the burial sack of a fellow prisoner, as it is cast into the sea. He uncovers a treasure on the Mediterranean island of Monte Cristo, acquires the title of Count, then seeks *not* revenge on those who had betrayed him ... but justice. One of these men is now the husband of Dante's beloved Mercedes. Author Dumas is adept at targeting the unbridled greed that ties the wealthy to those who rule—as Dantes puts it, "profiting by the suffering of others." The script was altered from the novel, allowing the former sweethearts to be reunited for a more upbeat, if abrupt, finish.

The Count of Monte Cristo **(1934) with Robert Donat (UA)**

Elissa and Georgia Caine (UA)

Landi provides Mercedes with emotional texture. She ably displays the unwavering love she holds for Dantes, as well as the perplexity when confronted with the man claiming to be The Count of Monte Cristo. In their scenes together, Landi and Donat show natural spontaneity and make a dynamic team. London's *Era* rated the film as "one of the year's ten best ... a personal triumph by Robert Donat. Elissa Landi achieves distinction by a subdued ease." *New York Times* summed up, "a first-class movie version of a classic novel. Donat's performance is lean, intelligent and quietly overwhelming. Elissa Landi gives the heroine in Monte Cristo a handsome and gallant look." *Photoplay* confirmed, "Elissa Landi is the perfect Mercedes." The film was among the box-office champs of 1934, and would have a successful reissue in 1938. Author James Robert Parish in his *Hollywood Players* (1976) wagered, "Probably the finest screen performance Elissa offered was as Mercedes, surrounded by a superlative cast and the excellent Robert Donat."[159]

The Count of Monte Cristo was Donat's American film debut. Despite his success, and offers from Warner Bros. for leads in *Anthony Adverse* and *Captain Blood*, Donat opted not to return to Hollywood, which he didn't really care for. "I never worked so hard in my life!" he said. "Why we didn't even stop in the afternoons for tea!" Prior to Donat and his wife's return to England, Elissa fêted the couple a lavish party. In London, Donat reflected, "Elissa's great fun. I owe all my Hollywood knowledge to her. We went around everywhere together and when there was time we rode and swam—my favorite sports. Elissa took me to a little Mexican restaurant, full of atmosphere, but the food was awful."[160]

Elissa played Mercedes with "subdued ease"(UA)

117

In 2020, during my conversation with Elissa's daughter Caroline Thomas, she stated that the relationship between her mother and Donat, wasn't exactly platonic. A romance developed. There exists several letters in which Elissa pours her heart out to Donat, before breaking off the relationship. Decades later, Caroline met with one of Donat's sons, who revealed this turn of events.[161] Apparently, affairs with leading ladies wasn't unusual turf for Donat. In the 1985 biography *Mr. Chips - The Life of Robert Donat*, author Kenneth Barrow confirmed that Donat enjoyed Elissa's "sense of humor and warm earthiness. The usual attentions he afforded his leading ladies were taken seriously by Miss Landi and an affaire [sic] developed between them." Barrow notes that once Donat and his wife were back home in London .... came the deluge.

> After they crossed the Atlantic, there was a volley of dramatic theatrical letters from Elissa. She felt herself 'an agnostic who had received proof of God's existence'. Her heart was apparently 'quite broken'. Within a few days she was writing on an altogether more prosaic level and then the letters stopped.[162]

Following a brief respite at Lake Tahoe, Landi headed to San Francisco with her mother for the opening of *The Count of Monte Cristo*. During a press interview, she stepped out onto a balcony at the Fairmont Hotel overlooking the bay. "I like it here," she said. "Lovely. It's nice to say 'lovely' and mean it." Her interviews with the *San Francisco Chronicle* were devoid of any comment about the film, *or* Donat. Obviously, a broken-heart kept the subject at bay. It also generated some bitterness. She confided to one San Francsico journalist, "I've been rotten in most of my screen parts. They're not interesting. I'm simply no good at doing a part that has not got a decided character to it ... color, reality, it must have or I have nothing to give it."[163]

<<>>

Several months later, Elissa targeted stars who were type-cast, obligated to maintain, as she put it, "their shadow personalities."

> I do not hold with an actress having a story molded to suit her adopted personality. It is not good acting, nor is it good sense. If I had allowed Hollywood to make me into, let us say, a sinuous siren, can you imagine what that would mean to me? My private life, my appearance in public, would be occasions to act. I'd have to slink across the room, with head bent forward, eyes half closed! There has been a conflict between me and Hollywood ever since I arrived. It was as to whether Hollywood should mold my destiny, or I would remain master of my fate. I know I did right in handling it myself.[164]

Elissa's battle with Schulberg-Feldman resurfaced in Superior Court that August. Abram Chasins sat next to Elissa during a three-day trial. Judge Lester Roth decided that regardless of the value of her agents' services, they had "put forth their best efforts to represent Miss Landi"—Schulberg-Feldman walked away with $7,400.[165] Elissa filed a cross-complaint that her contract with them be invalidated. Elissa's mother took the witness stand testifying that Columbia chief Harry Cohn had warned her daughter not to "let those flesh peddlers queer the picture." When Ralph Blum, the agency's lawyer, asked Caroline if she had discussed the case with anyone before the trial, she tersely replied, "Not any more than your clients have, Mr. Blum." Elissa burst out laughing at her mother's candor. Her friend Elsie Janis also took the stand, saying that *she* had been the one who introduced Landi to Cohn, before any contracts were signed. Judge Roth asked Janis if she had received anything as negotiator. Janis jokingly responded, "Nothing but a headache. I'm going to hold Elissa up for anything she has left after you all get through."[166] Judge Roth laughed along with the others, but denied Elissa's plea.

Ad Schulberg was the future ex-wife of Paramount producer Ben Schulberg. Ad herself was facing a tax lien from the U.S. government totaling $24,240. Their son Budd later revealed that Schulberg told his wife, "You know the trouble with you Ad? You love money. Well, there are other things in life." In Ben's case it was actress Sylvia Sidney. Following the hubbub of Elissa's trial, Ben and Sylvia invited Elissa to an informal dinner for Sidney's twenty-fourth birthday on August 8. The following year, Ben Schulberg would produce Landi's return to Broadway.

Amid all the financial strain, Elissa was prompted to organize Elissa Landi Corp. The Board of Directors consisted of Elissa, her secretary Mildred McClure, and mother Caroline. The three were authorized to handle all of Landi's business affairs.[167] The inclusion of Caroline, a lavish spender, seemed an odd choice, but as Elissa had turned over the household responsibilities to her mother, it seemed to be a practical, if dubious, step.

<<>>

***Enter Madame* (1935) with Cary Grant (Paramount)**

After weeks of negotiations (what *Variety* referred to as "considerable sparring") Landi signed with Paramount. It proved to be another short-lived career decision. She was still battling her agents as filming began on *Enter Madame*. She acquired the role opposite Cary Grant on her own, so it was a touchy situation when she encountered agent Feldman on the Paramount lot. Elissa offered him a smug, "Hello. Are you here to see about getting me a role in *Enter Madame*?"[168]

Enter Madame was dazzling to look at. The camerawork, editing, and Travis Banton costumes were satisfying to the eye. What the film lacked was a good script. The plot was an adaptation of a popular 1920 play. Scenarists Gladys Lehman and Charles Brackett, who would team with Billy Wilder to fuel such comedy classics as *Midnight* (1939) and *Ninotchka* (1939), provided a screenplay that lacked sophistication and wit. *New York Times* decided that the "hard-working cast ... were more animated than their dialogue."

Enter Madame immediately grabs attention as the Italian soprano Lisa della Robbia (Landi), playing Tosca, murders Baron Scarpia in Puccini's opera. When a candle flame accidently ignites the train of her elaborate gown, millionaire Cary Grant, an ardent fan, jumps from his opera box to the rescue. As the curtain falls he is knocked out. Amid the commotion the two fall into each other's arms only to ignite the flame of love. Landi appears to relish her role as a prima donna whose tantrums are embraced by an entourage of servants and admirers. Landi and Grant marry, but it isn't long before he is relegated to the role of official dog-walker for his wife's beloved Pekingese. After a hectic interlude of divorce proceedings and rumored affairs, the couple reunite. Grant realizes that he has missed the chaotic world that surrounds his diva-wife.

Motion Picture Daily enthused, "Miss Landi overacts beautifully." *Photoplay* concurred, "Landi, as a capricious prima donna, is at her best." Russian soprano Nina Koshetz coached Landi and dubbed her arias. One critic wagered that the magnificent voice of the 200-pound Koshetz, could never have come from the throat of the slender Elissa Landi. Elissa rated *Enter Madame* as "one of my pictures I really like. It is an excellent comedy and is well made." Boosting Elissa's confidence behind camera, was a new friend (and love interest) Jean Negulesco, an artist (and future director) who was technical advisor for *Enter Madame*'s opera scenes. *Stage* magazine praised Negulesco's work as, "The finest example of what a screened opera might be."

Opera diva Landi and Jean Negulesco

Cary Grant displayed his trademark charismatic charm. Decades later, Grant's friend Bea Shaw mentioned to him that she had seen *Enter Madame* on TV, he replied, "That wasn't me! That was some other fellow."[169] Grant may have been referring to his attempted suicide following the film's completion.[170] The English-born actor, like co-star Landi, would soon be dealing with his own divorce suit. Bea Shaw indicated that Grant admired Landi's talent, and especially her resistance to becoming a contract player. Grant probably picked up the vibe that Landi was already regretting her contract at Paramount. The studio announced that the two would reteam in *The Goddess*. When that didn't happen, Grant opted to go to MGM and the arms of Myrna Loy. Landi took several months off.

<<>>

Elissa's romance with Negulesco was described by his biographer Michelangelo Capua as a "short but intense liaison." Another author refers to Negulesco as Landi's "paramour."[171] They were frequently seen together during the first half of 1935. Negulesco escorted Landi (and occasionally her mother) to various Hollywood functions. The two were seen dining and dancing at the home of Norma Shearer and Irving Thalberg. Louella Parsons mentioned that Howard Hughes had thrown a huge dinner party in honor of Landi, but that there was no romantic attachment for the eccentric Texas tycoon, as "Elissa's best boyfriend, Jean Negulesco, was there."

December 27, 1935 - Landi between James Roosevelt and J.F.T. O'Connor

Amid a flurry of romance rumors, Landi took her divorce suit one step further. An interlocutory decree was granted on May 5, 1935, by Judge William S. Baird in Los Angeles. Elissa told Baird that she was called "the coldest woman in Hollywood," because of her faithfulness to her marital vows. Elissa's testimony was corroborated by her mother Caroline. The countess stated that her son-in-law was an "ogre," who called her daughter "ugly names."[172] It wasn't until May 1936 that Landi received her final decree from John Cecil Lawrence.

After divorce court, Landi landed in New York to do a radio broadcast with her former director Kenneth MacKenna (recently divorced from Kay Francis). The duo played the leads in A.A. Milne's *Michael and Mary*, a drama which one critic described as "a wallow in bigamist bliss." From there, Elissa headed to Washington D.C., telling reporters that she was too busy for love affairs. Her objective in D.C. was to visit J. F.T. O'Connor, who President Roosevelt had appointed as Comptroller of the Currency during the worst financial crisis in U.S. history. A month prior, she had thrown an elaborate party for him in Los Angeles. In turn, O'Connor hosted an tea reception in D.C. for Elissa, attended by a crowd of 600. A rumor began that the two were going to elope. O'Connor also arranged a meeting between Elissa and Vice-President James Nance Garner. She told Garner, "You know, if I met a man of your rank in Europe I would curtsy. So, permit me to do it now." Garner leaned over to kiss her hand, grinning, "Permit me to carry out the picture." Walter Winchell quashed the Landi-O'Connor elopement rumor, saying they parted ways so O'Connor's "political future wouldn't be hampered." O'Connor, who never married, was born in 1884.[173]

<<>>

Back at Paramount, Landi found herself in *Without Regret*, a low-budget remake of *Interference* (1928) loosely based on a 1927 British play that had boosted the career of Herbert Marshall. The synopsis centered on the wife

(Landi) of a prominent London physician (Paul Cavanagh), who assumed that her first husband (Kent Taylor) had lost his life in China. Truth is, he was now living under an assumed name. A former paramour of Taylor (Frances Drake) threatens the now bigamist wife with blackmail. Drake possesses old love letters written by Landi that would prove scandalous.

Cavanagh is rather cool and formal in his scenes with Landi, whereas the scenes between her and Taylor have definite chemistry, giving a bittersweet edge to the scenario. The demise of Drake's bitter character (she is poisoned) offers the necessary climactic sock. Drake and Taylor excel in portraying offbeat characters. Nonetheless, the situations feel more fictional than actual. David Niven, in his film debut, escorted Landi (his sister) to the train depot as the film opens. Niven later claimed that he was allotted one line, "Goodbye, my dear." He actually spoke several lines with a jaunty air as Landi sets out for "adventure."

Without Regret (1935) with Frances Drake (Paramount)

Reviews favored the performances more than the film. *Picture Play* summed up, "All this is heavy drama and not particularly interesting, except for excellent acting." *Photoplay* concluded that Taylor and Landi allowed *Without Regret* to succeed as "pleasant entertainment," and then wagged, "Landi unfreezes considerably in this one." A Dallas review thought the film "an overwrought hodge-podge ... despite its handsome mounting and its engaging players." The review mentioned Landi's upcoming return to Broadway, adding "If this is her farewell to the cinema, we are sorry."

<<>>

While columnists continued to focus on Landi's romantic attachments, she now claimed to be focused on remaining single. "Today I am free to be *myself*," she declared. With her divorce and money-matters in queue she felt more in charge. Elissa humored columnist Jack Grant when she stated, "I've never been a kept woman."[174] She admitted to having to support ex-husband Lawrence financially. "Money matters never did work out with him," she confessed. In 1935, Landi's main goal was to bring the remaining members of her family from England to California. With ample living quarters and acreage surrounding her home, she put her plan into motion. An unexpected $50,000 offer from a French film producer would secure Elissa's vision for a family reunited.

CHAPTER 9
Cloisters: A Family Reunited

Elissa christened her home at 1515 Amalfi Drive "The Cloisters." It was a seven acre sanctuary on the crest of Pacific Palisades, overlooking Hollywood on one side, and the cobalt blue Pacific Ocean on the other. An ornate grilled gate greeted Landi-seekers as they approached her Spanish Colonial home, surrounded by orange and lemon groves, terraced roses, maroon-hued petunias, poppies, and geraniums. Elissa enjoyed working outdoors in the California soil. One visitor noted, "She even has music with her gardening. A loud radio speaker commands her hillside ... symphonic music coming all the way from New York." When Elissa invited the press for a tour of her "Garden of Eden," one woman screamed and pointed to a 5-foot- long gopher snake. A few men began looking for a weapon. "Let it alone!" Elissa demanded. "It's perfectly harmless—and this is one garden without an apple tree!"[175]

A tennis court and bridle station revealed Landi's other outdoor passions. She routinely rode horseback along the miles of adjacent bridle paths owned by neighbor Will Rogers. Under these blessed circumstances, Elissa was compelled to make a confession—she danced barefoot on her moon-bathed terraces at night. "Sounds nutty," she said, "but it's fun!"[176]

Summer 1935, The Cloisters: Elissa, Caroline, Count Pi, Annie and Tony

The Cloisters

Cloister's living room

The Cloisters' immense living room reflected the outdoors, with the help of floral arrangements and mirrors. "Flowers, against a mirror background, have twice their usual effect," Landi enthused. The rooms were not only filled with flowers, but music, supplied by Elissa herself as she sat before either of her two pianos, or pipe organ. "My best moments of spiritual awareness," she confirmed, "come to me when I have keyboard conversations with Bach, Beethoven, Brahmas, Schubert, and Schumann."[177] In the basement, a printing press was installed so Elissa could publish her own verse. Mother Caroline, who managed the household schedule, occupied a cottage of her own that was connected to the main house. Another Cloister wing would soon be home to brother Anthony, his wife Annie, and their five-year-old daughter Elisabeth, now going by the nickname "Sooky".

Prior to leaving England, Anthony made a few headlines himself. On October 1, 1934, the thirty-one- year-old salesman had a collision on the London-Holyhead Road, north of the city. He swerved suddenly, lost control, and ended up hitting three cars in succession, one of them overturned. Anthony's face was cut and two ribs broken, before he collided with the last two vehicles. In a November court case, he was convicted of dangerous driving. His license was suspended. In January 1935, Anthony made a successful appeal to retain his license.[178] His career in sales required him to travel 40,000 miles annually. The episode, no doubt, was a motivating factor expediting his and wife Annie's sojourn to California. The following month, Anthony, Annie and Elisabeth voyaged to the U.S. on the *S.S. Champlain* ... for permanent residence.

Publisher Landi

Count Zanardi-Landi arrived in California in March 1935, after booking passage on the *S.S. President Hayes* from Genoa, Italy. The Count's native land was now under the fascist dictatorship of Benito Mussolini, who was edging towards aligning Italy with Hitler's anti-Semitic views. The ship's passenger list listed Zanardi-Landi as an Ex-Naval Captain. Retired from his 25-year career, the Count now looked out over the seascape of his California surroundings, and reflected, "I am making friends with this ocean."

Granted, he already had a congenial relationship with the Pacific while living in Vancouver. George Shaffer, of the *Chicago Tribune*, visited The Cloisters, noting how the Count nodded his head in agreement when Elissa declared, "This country is too wonderful to depart from. I am going to take American citizenship and the others in the family will probably do the same." When Shaffer asked if she would remarry, Landi replied, "That is asking too much of my Americanism."[179]

Landi's vision for a family reunited was celebrated with an elaborate Italian supper. The centerpiece for the dining table was a replica of a Venice canal. Tiny Italian houses rose up alongside the waters in which gondolas floated gracefully—a metaphor suggesting new beginnings for all concerned.

Dogs, cats, horses ... were stabilizing components in Landi's life

<<>>

In June 1935, Landi summed up, "My contract with Paramount expires in July and I am not going to sign again with them or any other studio. I simply can't continue working in pictures under my present set-up. I'm too unhappy. I spend most of my time fighting with men whose business it is to make me do what I don't want to do."[180] On July 10, Elissa took the first step towards becoming a U.S. citizen, signing a Declaration of Intention at a Los Angeles court. She stated, "I have cut myself off from the past and my European background." On that note, she portrayed *Elizabeth the Queen* on radio's *Rudy Vallee Show*, before sailing for Europe, to make back-to-back films in France and England.

Upon boarding the German liner *S.S. Bremen* on the evening of July 26, Elissa and her sister-in-law Annie observed what news reports referred to as "a howling Communist mob" along the pier. Over 1,000 demonstrators cheered as the German flag was torn down from the steamship stern. The protesters shouted, "Down with Hitler!" Scores of police officers rushed to the scene. The Nazi campaign against Jewish people was at the crux of the protest. As Elissa crossed the Atlantic, she came closer to the troubled shores of Europe, an experience that helped underscore her disassociation from her own roots. "The countries in Europe are so frightfully nationalistic," she admitted, "too much so."[181] (In 1943, Landi would tackle the nefarious ideology of Nazism in the critically acclaimed *Tomorrow the World* in which she played a Jewish school teacher.)

Soon after arriving in Paris, Elissa took an apartment, and began filming the historical romance *Koenigsmark*—a proposed $500,000 project. Director Leonce Perret had been intent on signing her. Landi received $50,000 to play the lead in both French and English versions. Director Perret directed a successful silent version of *Koenigsmark* (1923) and was highly regarded for his innovative, avant-garde style. As filming began, Perret fell ill. He died on August 12. Maurice Tourneur took his place. The fantastic plot and intrigue in *Koenigsmark* appealed to him. Tourneur, like Perret, had also directed silent films in America.

Koenigsmark (1935) (Capital)

Koenigsmark was adapted from the 1918 novel by Pierre Benoit. Landi played Aurore, a Grand Duchess locked into an arranged (and platonic) marriage with the Grand Duke of Lautenburg. It's not exactly a love-match. She refers to him as "the walrus." The unexpected demise of the Duke, places Lautenburg in the hands of Aurore. She rules with the aid of the Duke's overbearing brother Frederic (John Lodge). She also engages in romantic interludes with a French author (Pierre Fresnay) who is tutoring Frederic's young son. It is the tutor who solves the riddle of the Duke's ... *murder.* Set in the years prior to the outbreak of WWI, pageantry, political intrigue and romance coalesce into what novelist Graham Greene described as an "exciting, bogus, decorative film." Greene admired Landi's aristocratic heroine, observing, "Miss Elissa Landi has never before quite acted up to her beauty and obvious intelligence."[182] Watching the film in 2020, one is taken with the dazzling star-quality and piercing gaze that Landi generates in a vehicle that suited her talent. Director Tourneur's ability to do for Elissa Landi, what Hollywood failed to, would be cinema's loss.

Koenigsmark **with Pierre Fresnay (Capital)**

Writer Stiles Dickenson visited Pathe-Joinville studio, outside of Paris, during the six-week production. Tourneur was filming Landi's marriage to the Duke—an elaborate scene shot ten times in French, followed by four takes in English. Dickenson mentioned, "I was not surprised by Landi's French. I edged into a chair next to Elissa, who was a heavenly vision. Her bronze-gold hair and gray-green eyes need no other aids to set off their beauty." Dickenson bemoaned that the film was being shot in black-and white, as Landi was "one of the living arguments for color films." The fact she was making two films at once, and fluent in both languages, might explain Landi's generous salary. The film was released in France that December.

Paris reviews for *Koenigsmark* were ecstatic. *Le Petit Journal* enthused, "A veritable triumph! One is particularly impressed with the beautiful Elissa Landi." *Le Journal* said of Landi, "She triumphs as the heroine," then noted her "great sensibility in the sentimental parts" and "irresistible restrained emotion." *Figaro* agreed, "Elissa Landi deserves the highest praise. She is hostile without being stiff, proud without being haughty, distant without being cruel."

Illustrated London News (reviewing the English version, which was titled *Crimson Dynasty*) concurred with the Paris critics.

> Miss Elissa Landi moves gracefully through the hectic happenings. She draws a charming portrait of the lonely Princess, and cleverly suggests the gradual change from radiant girlhood to the authority of the later scenes. She has the necessary poise for the part, and plays it with a simple sincerity that is a valuable asset to a story apt to tax our credulity."

Koenigsmark **ad (Captial)**

Landi held her own against John Lodge's menacing Frederic. She allows Aurore to see through his maneuvers from the moment they meet. Pierre Fresnay (a favorite actor of Alec Guinness) offers a compelling performance in a complex role. He is the perfect romantic *vis-a-vis* for Landi's determined heroine.

<<>>

As Elissa completed her work with Tourneur, she was summoned by Douglas Fairbanks Jr., who had launched his own independent production company Criterion Films, in London. He was filming an adaptation of the 1913 English romance novel *The Amateur Gentleman*, which takes place during England's Regency period (1811-1820). In his 1988 autobiography *Salad Days*, Fairbanks detailed, "We needed a lovely-looking, experienced leading lady with a salable name. Luckily we found the much-admired Elissa Landi at liberty." Naturally, Landi was enthused about working with Fairbanks.

Doug's long romance with actress Gertrude Lawrence, in his own words, had "almost completely petered out." Since filing for divorce from Joan Crawford in 1933, Doug and "Gee" (as he called Lawrence) were a steady duo. In a 1998 interview with journalist James Bawden, Fairbanks elaborated, "There wasn't a bigger stage star at the time, but she wasn't photogenic. Had a big, crooked nose, eyes weren't right. I fell completely in love. We had a time of it, but ultimately her high living threatened to bankrupt both of us."[183] Doug began looking elsewhere.

> I now found myself making a deliberate off-stage play for my new leading lady, Elissa Landi. Usually I kept business and pleasure carefully apart. In this case, it was all more for the fun of the game than anything else. Elissa was intensely serious about almost everything—the weather, the price of eggs, her costumes. She was oppressively intellectual—a characteristic that her Hollywood colleagues reported was sometimes off-putting.

Although she could be excellent company and was well informed, she lacked the sense of humor I knew and liked best.[184]

The press wagered that the co-stars were up to more than just "the fun of the game." "Filmdom Hears Doug Jr. to Wed Elissa Landi," read one headline. Doug filled Landi's dressing room with flowers every day, and was "constantly in her company when away from the studio." Perhaps feeling less vulnerable, Elissa stood her ground. As the film wrapped, one observer noted the duo at lunch having "intermittent arguments about nonsensical matters." Fairbanks sent word to friends in Hollywood that he was *not* engaged to Landi. Elissa's own response to the rumors? "Absolute rubbish!"[185]

Douglas Fairbanks Jr. woos Elissa in *The Amateur Gentleman* (1936)
(Criterion)

Amateur Gentleman began filming in October. As Lady Cleone, Landi is wooed by Barnabus Barty (Fairbanks), who is masquerading as a Regency "buck"—an amateur gentleman. Barty is mixing into society to find an aristocrat thief. He wants to clear his imprisoned father, an ex-boxer, from a crime he didn't commit. The real culprit is Cleone's fiancé Louis (Basil Sydney). At an opportune moment Barty declares his love for Cleone, and reveals the truth about his "masquerade." Together, they visit his father in prison and arrange for his escape. Cleone breaks her engagement to Louis, before a whirlwind of murder, a carriage chase, and clever ruse send her now ex-fiancé to the gallows. *The Amateur Gentleman* does a good job of exposing the sham of wealth and aristocracy. The humanity of Barty's character is revealed throughout, especially in a scene where he sees a man abusing a horse. Barty gives the guy a well-deserved wallop. The conscious-stricken man apologizes. Barty offers him a few shillings for a beer, and oats for the horse.

The Amateur Gentleman **with Coral Browne and Douglas Fairbanks Jr.**
(Courtesy of Jenny Paxson)

When she wasn't before the camera, Landi kept busy embroidering a tapestry. The borders were decorated with signatures of all her family, including a misspelled version from her niece and namesake, Elisabeth. Before the task was complete, tragedy struck The Cloisters. On the evening of November 16, Doug and Elissa were guests on a BBC radio broadcast offering a scene from *The Amateur Gentleman*. The following evening, Elissa received news that her mother Caroline died unexpectedly. Elissa's response to the press was heartfelt. "I have lost not only my mother but my greatest friend. I hope I shall never forget the lesson of courage she has always taught me."[186]

Elissa put in double-time, working far into the night, to finish *Amateur Gentleman*. On November 21, Landi and her sister-in-law left Waterloo Station in London en route for New York. Fairbanks Jr. and producer Marcel Hellman saw them off. Elissa and Annie arrived in New York on November 27. It was reported that from there, they flew to Los Angeles. Columnist Mollie Merrick paid tribute to Countess Landi, saying she "had a vital and forceful personality, and a generous and fun-loving soul, which made her one of the great figures in life here."

In 2020, I had a telephone conversation with Elissa's niece Sooky (now going by Suki Landi Sennett). It was Suki who discovered her grandmother Caroline's body at The Cloisters. "I found her on the bathroom floor," she told me. "I screamed and ran away." She heard "fits of commotion" in the aftermath, as the adults dealt with the situation. Caroline had died of a heart attack. The girl who made this heartbreaking discovery, a month-and-a-half shy of her sixth birthday, had no female presence to comfort her. Her mother Annie was with Elissa, and Landi's faithful secretary Mildred McClure, who Suki especially liked, was spending time in Dallas prior to a sojourn to New York to meet her employer. Instead, Mildred returned post-haste to Los Angeles. Suki mentioned that Mildred had her own wing at their home, and was a key ingredient to The Cloisters' success.

During our conversation, Suki fondly recalled her grandmother's "wonderful cooking" and buoyant personality. "She was quite a character!"

Suki admitted. "Caroline ran through money like nobody's business! She married Pi for *his* money!"[187] Suki pointed out, "I was told by my mother that Caroline had run through his money as she had with Elissa's Hollywood earnings."[188] So much for Elissa Landi Corp.!

❮❮❯❯

Amateur Gentleman premiered in London on January 20, 1936. *Motion Picture Daily* cheered that there was "plenty of dramatic action ... fist fights, a helter-skelter coach chase ... definite entertainment values for American audiences." On that note, Fairbanks Jr. boarded the *S.S. Majestic* for New York carrying a print of the film and high hopes for success. Released in April, *Film Daily* summed up, "Young Doug gives an excellent performance. He puts up a fast pair of fists in the bare-knuckle fight against a gigantic bruiser." *Screenland* found Landi to be "a picturesque heroine." Cleveland critic W. Ward Marsh, thought the adaptation "a strong one, having excellently created scenes ... and a nice interweaving of love interest, melodrama and suspense. The playing is of a high order." *Variety* had the temerity to complain that "effeminate actions of the English fops ... and the prissiness of the male extras ... makes the film doubtful for American consumption." Though *The New York Times* bemoaned the "liberally altered version" of the original novel, it praised the "considerable skill of the cast" and acknowledged "not too bad a beginning for Criterion Pictures."

Fairbanks offered dash and humor to Barnabus Barty, and easily involves the viewer in Barty's quest to solve a mystery. He comes across as *genuine*, demonstrating that Barty was a man with a good heart (a rare commodity among screen heroes). Even his much publicized bare-knuckled boxing match of flesh-and-muscle (he wins with a double-punch) demonstrates skill rather than bravado. Landi carries an engaging sense of humor, coupled with a touching display of anguish regarding Barty's plight, and that of her gambling-addicted brother (Hugh Williams). Fairbanks and Landi connect to make an appealing on-screen couple.

141

Landi admitted that her experience in Europe was a positive one. "The acting over there seems more *real*," she said. "They have deeper roots in tradition and know instinctively how to depict human emotions. The experience broadened me, and I feel that I will be able to do better work having had it."[189] Fairbanks was pleased with *Amateur Gentleman*, which did fairly well in the European market—more profitable than his following two films for Criterion. His affection for the film translated into indignation during his 1998 hour-long phone interview with James Bawden. "What!" cried Fairbanks, "You've never seen *The Amateur Gentleman* with Elissa Landi?"[190]

<< >>

Prior to *The Amateur Gentleman*, it was announced that Landi would return to Broadway in December for producer B.P. Schulberg's production of *Tapestry in Gray*, by Martin Flavin (a future Pulitzer-prize winning novelist), and co-starring Melvyn Douglas. After reconnecting with family and mourning the loss of her mother, Elissa headed to New York for rehearsals at the Shubert Theatre. How did she feel about getting back to Broadway? "Here I am," she stated, "rehearsing madly and loving it. I think we've got a great play. And I read it over a year ago. I've traveled over 9,000 miles in less than six months to be able to play the role—so you see I must want to do it badly. I hope the play runs on and on." *Tapestry in Gray* had shades of *A Farewell to Arms*. Landi was once again cast as a nurse during WWI.

In 1977, cast member Cornelia Bell commented on the tryouts. "There were hundreds of people out in front of the theater ... all unemployed. One-quarter were probably legitimate actors." Six years into the Great Depression, people were still desperate for jobs. Bell remembered a woman coming out of the casting room, jesting, "Well, I've got my part and I still have my clothes on." (Most likely she was the play's designated "street walker"). Bell was cast as the governess of Landi and Douglas' son (played by seven-year-old Richard "Dick" Van Patten—whose career would span seven decades).

142

When the governess has to report that the son is injured, Bell thought it would be her "big moment"—and burst into tears during the first rehearsal. Playwright Flavin raised an eyebrow and said, "That's enough of that; this is Elissa Landi's scene, not yours."[191]

Tapestry in Gray (1935-36)- **caricatures of Melvyn Douglas, Landi and Minor Watson**

The costly production consisted of 37 scenes with numerous flashbacks. The play opens with Iris (Landi) contacting a psychologist in order to help her surgeon husband Erik (Melvyn Douglas) who suffers from aphasia (brain disorder). In a flashback, Iris and Erik's son (Van Patten) is hurt in an auto accident. The remainder of the play details the demise of Erik, whose attempt to save his son had failed. Iris feels responsible for all the mishaps, and attempts to redeem herself.

The play was directed by Hollywood's Marion Gering, who had helmed several Sylvia Sidney films. Sidney herself was in attendance opening night, along with Henry Fonda, Una Merkel, and Errol Flynn. Afterward, a celebration at a posh supper club found Elissa sitting between President Roosevelt's eldest son James, and J.F.T. O'Connor. As reviews came in, critics were mostly harsh. John Mason Brown, for the *New York Post*, described it as "an elusive, pretentious ... endless bore." Brown, who had much admired Landi's performance in *A Farewell to Arms*, felt that now she was "more camera-conscious, than audience conscious." Critic Burns Mantle wagered, "Miss Landi gives technically a fine performance, but the play swamps her. As it also swamps Douglas." *Tapestry in Gray* lasted three weeks, and was considered the year's most expensive flop. While critics favored Melvyn Douglas' portrayal, he later summed up the experience as, "I got too big for my britches."[192]

<<>>

In February, Landi and her secretary Mildred returned to California, via New Orleans for some sightseeing. At home they were greeted by camera-crews. Brother Anthony had co-founded a film company, Sentential Productions. His first feature film, as associate producer, was *What Becomes of the Children?* (1936). The low-budget exploiter, starring Joan Marsh, focused on the woes of broken marriages. Ads for this "Adults Only" offering referred to it as "A Sensational Sex Drama." The film implied that children of divorce, upon reaching adulthood, are more likely to face the electric chair! Apparently, Elissa supported this venture. Tony used The Cloisters to establish the affluence of the family in question.[193] He paid off a screenwriter with one of his sister's horses![194] Tony was also helping actress Jean Muir establish Theatre Workshop, which was designed to help young actors establish experience before going into films. He helped Muir organize, incorporate, and sell stock, a skill and interest that Tony would successfully employ throughout his life. His tie to Sentential Productions, however, was short-lived. Anthony Landi's next try as associate producer wasn't until ... 1948.

Elissa was now more involved with managing The Cloisters. She admitted, "I have gotten thinner since mother died. But, somehow, I'm more flexible, too. I lost twelve pounds at the time of her death and knew I must get a hold on myself. Now that I have to do everything myself, I honestly think my brain is more flexible. While she lived, I never attended to anything."[195]

1936 - Simpatico: Landi at the piano, accompanies Nino Martini

For romantic diversion, Elissa was now spending time with tenor Nino Martini. From Verona, Italy, Nino was filming the musical-farce *The Gay Desperado* (1936). He was determined to establish a double career, both in Hollywood and at the Metropolitan Opera. When asked about Landi, Martini waxed poetic: "Elissa Landi? Ah, yes. She is my favorite! She has something that sets her apart. She is beautiful, yes, but it is more than that. I think it must be a quality of mind. She is different from all the others."[196] When asked if they would marry, he smiled, "I like people, but I don't get engaged to them." When Elissa was asked the same question she fumed, "I'm not engaged to anyone! When I am, I'll be the first to admit it. I'll shout it from the housetops! I'm continually being reported engaged. Worst of all, it's bad publicity for me. I don't believe my public likes to believe that I am engaged to one man one day and another the next. That's the sort of thing that starts all kinds of impossible rumors."[197] Nino was on hand to witness this tirade, and the reporter noted that the "liquid-eyed" tenor seemed "somewhat aghast at her vehemence."

Fact was, Landi's "quality of mind" was unsettled by a difficult decision she had made. In August 1936, MGM producer Irving Thalberg encouraged Elissa to do exactly what she vowed *never* to do again—sign another long-term studio contract.

CHAPTER 10
"Hollywood-I Wasted Seven Good Years of My Life There"

M-G-M

Producer Irving Thalberg had championed Landi's move to MGM early on. In the fall of 1933 her MGM contract was all set to go, but a clause that limited Landi's access to Thalberg made her skeptical. She refused to sign. Thalberg felt that the clause in question was a maneuver by Louis B. Mayer to stonewall his decision to hire Landi. He wrote in his journal, "I regret this, as I believe Landi could have been developed into a real star."[198]

On September 14, 1936, producer Thalberg died unexpectedly. He had been in fragile health, but still it came as a shock to the film industry. He was only thirty-seven. As the news sank in, it must have been a sobering experience for Elissa. Without Thalberg there for support what were her chances for significant roles?

<<>>

Mad Holiday **(1936) with Edmund Lowe (MGM)**

MGM announced that Landi would co-star with William Powell and Myrna Loy in a sequel to the popular comedy-mystery *The Thin Man* (1934). To acclimate her to the genre, she began filming *Mad Holiday*, a spoof of detective films starring Edmund Lowe. Lowe played a popular film-sleuth who was fed up playing the same role over and over. He tells his producer, "I've tripped over my last corpse!" For Elissa, life reflects art. She plays an author. Using the *nom de plume* Peter Dean (portrayed on book covers as an elderly man with a long beard), she, unbeknownst to Lowe, created his on-screen character. After complaining that Dean's "brains have gone to his whiskers," Lowe opts for a long sea voyage.

Learning that Lowe is escaping Hollywood, Landi books passage on the same boat. The two of them, after being handcuffed and drugged, try to solve an onboard murder involving a missing diamond. Landi looks svelte and lovely amid the madcap goings-on, and as *Motion Picture* magazine put it, "played her part with spirit and charm." She and Lowe connect with simpatico. But was *Mad Holiday* seaworthy? Despite an overabundance of plot (and dubious characters) *The New York Times* generously described the film as an "engaging variation on the 'whodunit?'" A tipsy ZaSu Pitts, along with publicity hound Ted Healy and his photographer "stooge," boosted the hilarity in an attempt to keep things afloat. *Harrison Reports* indicated that box-office was only "fair" for what *Motion Picture Herald* described as "hokum-packed satire ... geared for those not too choosey."

At this juncture Landi went from the ridiculous to the sublime. *After The Thin Man*, nominated for Best Screenplay in 1937 and yielding a profit of $1.5 million, is considered by aficionados as the best of the series. London novelist/critic Graham Greene indicated that *After the Thin Man* was "rather superior to the first ... not thirty seconds is left unfilled by an expert and amusing gag. One is grateful for pictures like this."[199] As Myrna Loy said in her memoir, "We were lucky with *After the Thin Man*." Elissa began filming in early October, after Loy and Powell returned from location shooting in San Francisco.

On screen, detective Nick Charles (Powell) is once again nudged out of retirement to help out wife Nora (Loy), whose cousin Selma (Landi) is in a jam. Selma, who resides with her aristocratic aunt (Jessie Ralph) in San Francisco, begs Nick to locate her straying husband Robert (Alan Marshal) who is philandering with a nightclub singer. James Stewart shows up as David, an old flame of Selma's, who is still madly in love with her. David attempts to pay off Robert if he promises to leave Selma for good. Robert leaves ... with the help of a bullet in his back. A confused Selma isn't quite sure if she pulled the trigger herself. Nick Charles, as expected, finds clues to zero in on the guilty one.

A quirky mix of ex-cons, boozers and social outcasts add color to the proceedings. Lawrence J. Quirk felt that Landi gave "weight and substance to the melodramatics." James Stewart was embarrassed by his own performance. He later commented, "I was ludicrous. I think people must have burst out

149

laughing." Stewart underestimated himself. It was a jarring revelation to learn that *he* was the guilty one. His unexpected hysterics at the finish inadvertently gave audiences a chuckle when a crackpot psychiatrist blurts out, "Good heavens, I was right. The man *is* crazy!" When Nora first witnesses Selma's hysterics—Loy herself offered a priceless reaction for the camera, indicating that Selma had a loose screw. Overall, the film was buoyed by the private jokes and comic asides that Nick and Nora toss back-and-forth. Thanks to director Woody Van Dyke MGM had another gem on their hands.

"Registering deep distress" in *After the Thin Man* **(1936)**

After the Thin Man **(1936) with Myrna Loy and William Powell (MGM)**

Critics were impressed with Landi's contribution to *After the Thin Man*: "Elissa Landi proves how charming an actress can be even when perpetually registering deep distress"; "Miss Landi manages restraint in a difficult role"; "The return of Elissa Landi. Her beautiful voice, exquisite diction and refinement must never be lost to us again." One theater manager offered a plea to MGM, via *Motion Picture Herald*, that read: "Now that you have Elissa Landi, why not give her a break? If any studio can make a star of her, you can."

Elissa was asked if she was satisfied with the roles the studio was offering. "Good heavens, no," she replied. "Look at that awful part in *After the Thin Man*. They said it was a big picture—well, what of it? My part wasn't big. But I've decided I'll not let the studio say I'm difficult, so I do every role they give me and say nothing."[200] (In 1943, Elissa indicated that out of all her films she "had the most fun" making *After the Thin Man*.)

**Fun on the set. MGM's Nelson Eddy sings "Ah, Sweet Mystery of Life,"
to the delight of Elissa, Myrna Loy, and James Stewart**

<<>>

Tenor Nino Martini was a frequent visitor to the MGM set, as well as Elissa's home. Their attraction centered on music (and horseback riding). Martini found Americans out of sync with aspects of his Italian roots. "Everybody in Verona sings," he enthused. "Life would not be life there, if people did not make music. Everybody hums or sings or plays the concertina. Why are Americans not like that, too? They would get so much more out of life, be so much more happy."

At the end of October, Elissa saw Nino off at the airport prior to his concert tour on the east coast. She then flew to San Francisco for the opening of the opera season. A die-hard Wagner fan, she was able to attend *Götterdämmerung* with Kirsten Flagstad and Lauritz Melchior. Martini had once been asked, with Landi present and listening, who his favorite composer was. His favorite roles were Arturo in Bellini's *I Puritani*, and Rodolfo in Puccini's *La Boheme*. But, with Elissa staring him down, he was at a loss for words, then diplomatically answered, "Wagner." His repertoire neglected the German maestro, except for one 1937 broadcast when he offered an aria from *Die Meistersinger* ... in Italian. Elissa was less than happy. "Miss Landi cannot think I am right," Nino said. "'Wagner in Italian!' she cried. 'How bad! How terrible!'" To make amends while on tour, Nino sent Elissa bouquets of gardenias. This prompted columnist Ed Sullivan to predict, "Nino Martini will pop the question to Elissa Landi any second!" When Nino was asked if was married, he answered with his easy-going smile, "I don't know!" Elissa's response to her "pending" betrothal vacillated between, "I might. I honestly don't know yet," and "I've been married, and I don't want to divorce again."[201]

Prior to making yet another whodunit, Landi and MGM leading man Robert Montgomery starred in Lux Radio's comedy *Grand Duchess and the Waiter* (an adaptation of a 1924 Parisian play). Landi portrayed Grand Duchess Xenia, who, in order to maintain her "nobility" after Bolsheviks run her out of Russia, succumbs to selling her jewelry at a Swiss hotel. While there, she is confronted with the clumsy waiter Albert (Montgomery).

Montgomery's flippancy melts the arrogance of Landi's Duchess, and the two declare their love for each other. They team well in this fresh and amusing trifle. *Variety* decided Landi and Montgomery "did nicely ... in a thin story that moved along with enough zip to hold."

1936 with NinoMartini; Martini at the Metropolitan Opera

It was a reunion for Landi and Lux host Cecil B. DeMille, who commented on her "remarkable talent" being a factor in casting her in *The Sign of the Cross*. It was too bad that MGM didn't team Landi, who preferred dramatic roles, with Montgomery in his next film *Night Must Fall*, for which he received an Academy Award nomination. (Rosalind Russell co-starred in a role that held complexities beneath an icy surface). Montgomery was president of Screen Actors Guild (SAG), which Landi regarded with unbridled enthusiasm. Seeking a closed shop, SAG went on strike in May 1937. After Montgomery got the cooperation of a reluctant Louis B. Mayer, he announced the Guild's victory to a rally of several thousand at the Hollywood Legion stadium. A San Francisco correspondent reported, "Cheering lustily near me was the petite Elissa Landi, the blood of the Habsburgs flushing her face with a sense of the power of organization."

Landi supervised as technical advisor for *A Day at the Races* (1937)

Early in 1937, Landi jumped at the chance to assist director Sam Wood in the Marx Bros. comedy *A Day at the Races* (1937). Landi's expertise with horses enabled her to advise Wood on derby sequences, as a technical advisor. Her own prize-winning champion horse Tristan was featured in the production. Tristan had already brought her a certain amount of glory when he entered horse shows and jump contests.

<<>>

Having known each other for six years, Elissa and Myrna Loy spent time together on and off the MGM lot. While they were strolling along together, a friend of Loy's came up and remarked, "I didn't know you two were friends!" Landi supplied the rejoinder, "Of course we're friends. Why, Myrna has stood the supreme test. She has read my books!" Since late summer of 1936, author Landi had announced the pending publication of *Today the Rebels*, in which she predicted another American revolution. Her publisher was "anxiously waiting" the final proofs. By April 1937, the book was mentioned as "about to be published." It wasn't. The book's demise added to a mounting list of disappointments that would motivate Landi to take her career in new directions.

The 13th Chair (1937) with Ralph Forbes (MGM)

Elissa indicated the kind of role she *really* wanted. As shown in *Koenigsmark*, the costume drama was well suited to what she had to offer the screen. "I'd like to have the lead in *Prisoner of Zenda*," she told New Orleans correspondent Mel Washburn. According to Washburn, Landi had been considered for the role. Shortly after the interview it was confirmed that Madeline Carroll landed the part of Princess Flavia in David O. Selznick's production. Instead of Selznick and *Zenda*, MGM carelessly placed Elissa

Landi at the nadir of her film career. She was once again relegated to fourth-billing—but this time in a programmer titled *The 13th Chair*. Her name was placed below Dame May Whitty, Madge Evans and Lewis Stone.

The 13th Chair, adapted from a 1916 play, was filmed twice before. The 1937 remake, helmed by veteran director George B. Seitz (who had also directed *Mad Holiday*), was a definite improvement. Running a brisk 66 minutes, this moody murder mystery centered on a medium (Whitty) who holds a séance with thirteen guests/suspects. As the lights dim, Whitty reaches out to the spirit world. During her trance, one guest suddenly dies. A knife that did the deed is found lodged into the ceiling. A police inspector (Stone) arrives on the scene to investigate. Evidence points to the medium's own daughter (Evans). Landi played Helen Trent, who Evans is shielding. Landi, in turn, is shielding her own husband (Ralph Forbes).

Landi's role consisted of a dozen-or-so lines, and was confined to what the *San Francisco Chronicle* fleetingly described as one among a "strange assortment of characters." The review determined that the film was "an exciting and chilling hour, highly recommended." Dame May Whitty stole the acting honors. While the cast offers her solid support, it is Whitty who makes the film worth watching. Landi's Hollywood swansong was the first film in England to be slapped with an "H" certificate (Horrific)—unsuitable for those under the age of 16.

With nothing else in queue, MGM cast Elissa in *Hollywood Party*, a Technicolor musical short in which she hosts an Asian-themed garden party. The only talents worth watching in this 21-minute mixed bag were tenor Joe Morrison's melodic "South Sea Island Magic," and the Jones Boys (aka The Red Caps) who used harmony and vocal invention to imitate musical instruments. The film's shortcomings were sidetracked by brief glimpses of celebrity guests: Clark Gable, Joan Bennett, Joe E. Brown, and Freddie Bartholomew. *Box Office* wagered, "Even an abundance of talent such as this does not always guarantee entertainment." *Film Daily* was more optimistic, saying *Hollywood Party* "moves with a brisk tempo, and is sure-fire with any type of audience."

Hollywood Party (1937) (MGM)

‹ ‹ › ›

Since 1925 Metro boasted having "more stars than there are in heaven."[202] Just where did Elissa Landi fit into this constellation? Trade publications designated that Landi was not a MGM star, but a "featured player." Featured players supported the studio's designated major stars. Since her arrival in Hollywood, several journalists indicated that Landi would never reach full stardom due to the fact that she "had brains." Los Angeles correspondent Alice L. Tildesley confronted Landi about the accusation, to which Landi carefully pointed out,

> I don't believe Joan Crawford could have raised herself from
> her first performances in program pictures to her present place on
> the screen if she had no brains. Norma Shearer did the hard work
> that brought her to the top ranks. You can't play Shakespeare so
> well that you are acclaimed by critics unless you work, and work

hard. Because Jean Harlow plays so many of the giddy, dumb Dora roles it's sometimes said that she hasn't any brains. But Jean wouldn't last if she hadn't a mind. Jean's performances, too, are always deft and delightful. You don't achieve her skill without work.[203]

The "deft and delightful" Harlow would pass away of uremic poisoning on June 7, 1937, at the age of 26. Hollywood was in shock. Elissa attended the memorial service at Forest Lawn, along with numerous stars: Harlow's current suitor William Powell, Clark Gable, Norma Shearer, Joan Crawford, Kay Francis, Myrna Loy and over 200 other celebrities. Jeanette MacDonald sang "Indian Love Call," and broke down weeping. Nelson Eddy rushed to her side, helping to complete the song. Eddy closed the service with one of Harlow's other favorites, "Ah, Sweet Mystery of Life."[204] Jeanette and Nelson both knew that Harlow was a devoted fan, hence the request that they sing— and the ensuing tears.

Fall 1936. On the set of the Technicolor version of *Maytime* with MacDonald and Eddy.

Nelson clowning with Elissa's fur, during the black-and-white version. Did she tickle his fancy? (MGM)

There are indications that Landi's own acquaintance with Nelson Eddy was more than casual. Eddy could easily have been a factor she considered when she decided to sign with MGM. From the moment she arrived, the two were often seen lunching together at the studio commissary. Per Nelson Eddy's invitation, Elissa had been a frequent visitor on the set of *Maytime*, considered by many to be the best of the MacDonald-Eddy operettas. *Maytime* began filming in August 1936—in Technicolor. In October, the production, nearly half-completed, was scrapped. Elissa's visits continued that fall while the final black-and-white version was before the camera. *Maytime* was completed just before Nelson's concert tour in January. He arrived at Salt Lake City's Mormon Tabernacle to an adoring audience that was three-fourths women. *Utah Daily Chronicle* headlined: "Nelson Eddy is Besieged - Coeds Swarm About Adonis." From then on, Elissa's romantic diversion remained focused on Nino. Rumors of their pending marriage would fuel gossip columns for two more years.

Hearst news ran their first nationwide annual radio poll in January

1937. The top two favorites for "Best Male Vocalist (Concert or Opera)" reflected Elissa's taste in men: Nelson Eddy (first place) and Nino Martini (second place). Mementos from Landi's liaisons with these two singers were mentioned in her 1944 novel *The Pear Tree*. The story's deceased protagonist, Malvina, had kept photographs of two men over the intervening years. The portrait of a handsome blond was signed: "It was fun, Vina - Nelson." The other photo was signed, "My best wishes - Nino."

<<>>

Landi revisited Lux Radio for DeMille's presentation of Booth Tarkington's masquerade, *Monsieur Beaucaire*, costarring Leslie Howard. Before Howard headed home for England, he had the cheek to name those he considered to be the 10 "most intelligent" women in Hollywood. He mentioned Elissa, and former co-stars Kay Francis and Bette Davis. Director Dorothy Arzner and columnist Sheilah Graham also made the list. He knew all these women personally. "Having brains" apparently, was no detriment to these women's careers.

In July 1937, it was official. Landi was returning to Broadway that Fall to co-star with Vincent Price in the Hungarian play *Jean*. She rhapsodized for the *Jersey Journal*, "I decided to hie me to New York to rehearsals of a stage play ... and then the fun will begin. I'm ever so pleased about the whole thing. I shall miss my horse and my dogs and cats. I shall miss my friends. But ... ." It seemed doubtful that MGM's announcement of Landi co-starring with Powell and Loy in the madcap comedy *Double Wedding* would come to fruition. As Powell's ex-wife, Landi would have received 10th billing! Katharine Alexander inherited the role, which consisted of one scene with Loy which lasted exactly *one* minute. The cruelty of the powers that be at MGM (ie. Louis B. Mayer) was a deciding factor in Landi leaving her film career behind.

Landi's "last hurrah" to Hollywood before flying to New York, was portraying Rosalind in *As You Like It* for the CBS Shakespeare Cycle. By August 25, she and Vincent Price were in rehearsals for *Jean*, soon to be re-titled *The Lady Has a Heart*. The tryout took place at Shubert Theatre in New Haven on September 20, and was "fairly well received." 20th-Century Fox was already onboard to make a film version with William Powell and Annabella, titled *The Baroness and the Butler*.

"THE LADY HAS A HEART"

a comedy by
LADISLAUS BUS-FEKETE

with

VINCENT   ELISSA
PRICE   LANDI

HILDA SPONG · LUMSDEN HARE
AND A DISTINGUISHED CAST
Adaptation by Edward B. Roberts
Staged by MR. PHILLIPS   Settings by MR. BARRATT

SHUBERT THEATRE
NEW HAVEN
Three Days Only Beginning
MONDAY, SEPTEMBER 20th

Fall 1937 - *The Lady Has a Heart* with Vincent Price

On Saturday evening September 25, Broadway's Longacre Theatre welcomed *The Lady Has a Heart*, which focused on royal affairs—political and romantic. Price played Jean, a man servant to the Premier of Hungary. During a political upheaval Jean represents the opposition's Socialist Party. His eloquence as a speaker moves the Hungarian Parliament to the point of revolution. Landi was Countess Katinka, the Premier's haughty married daughter. As expected, Jean captures Katinka's heart, and, as the critic for *Brooklyn Daily Eagle* pointed out, "Mr. Price has one opportunity to kiss Miss Landi. He makes the most of it; so does she." Following Katinka's divorce, Jean drops out of politics to engage in matrimonial bliss. The review brusquely summed up: "And that's all there is to it."

The first-night audience offered a standing ovation, but *Variety* noted an "absence of effective comedy." The review felt that Price was "good enough" and that Landi "showed spirit as his titled lover." *New York Post* complained, "Elissa Landi ... acts with more energy than effect; indeed with a violence which sometimes threatens to be dismembering." Another critic felt that Landi "delivered her lines as if she were taking pot shots at the audience." Soon after the play closed, theater critic Louise Mace came to the defense of both Landi and the play.

> *The Lady Has a Heart* was a diverting and ingenious comedy. Miss Landi exercised infinite skill in pointing up the mental and emotional complexity, so that the spectators were amused while the countess was happily astounded at her crash through the social barriers. This is creative acting. Miss Landi's role was accomplished with crystal clarity and rhythmic dexterity. The barren New York season is weakened by the play's untimely demise.[205]

Critic Burns Mantle described Price as, "A likeable lad ... with limitations that have more to do with lack of experience than anything else." After Price's rave notices working with Helen Hayes in *Victoria Regina* (which ran for two years), he was fit to be tied. Accolades from *The New York Times* and *Commonweal* ("He is one of the most promising American actors") weren't enough. Price reflected years afterward that Elissa was "a wide-eyed wonder of womanly perfection. Even in her maturity, she had a young girl's stance and stare. I felt she hid a certain shyness by pretending to act, which she did rather diffidently and not too well. One couldn't help liking Elissa."[206] Price's assessment of Landi was rooted in his own negative reviews. Brooks Atkinson for *The New York Times* found Price's performance "monotonous." "For all his charms," wrote Atkinson, "Mr. Price is going to be a dull actor unless he can learn how to give himself to a play." "It almost broke my heart," sobbed Price, "When you are a big success in the beginning of your career, it's difficult to swallow adverse criticism."[207]

At the end of November, *The Lady Has a Heart*, boosted by reduced ticket prices, transferred to the 46th Street Theater, where it closed after a total of 91 performances on December 14. It was reported, "Vincent Price's illness is the reason."[208] Critic Louise Mace also mentioned the "unfortunate" and "sudden" closure due to the illness of Landi's leading man. Undoubtedly, it was the leading man's wounded ego that was to blame. At the behest of Orson Welles, Price was already rehearsing for Mercury Theater's revival of *The Shoemaker's Holiday* which previewed at the end of the month, and ran for 69 performances.[209]

Three months was certainly a fair run for Broadway, and Elissa was not discouraged. Sylvia Sidney and Henry Fonda had less successful returns to Broadway that season. Sidney's *To Quito and Back* folded after 46 performances. Fonda's *Blow Ye Winds* (even with cut-rate tickets) lasted 36 performances. It was Fonda's last play for 11 years. Critics were harsh, making barbs about "movie actors" attempting to be stage worthy. Only Elissa and Sylvia were determined to hang on. Sylvia complained that Hollywood was a "false world" and bought a farm in New Jersey. Within a year, Elissa would follow suit.

March 1938 - *Empress of Destiny* lasted 5 performances

Cinema's "Empress of Emotion" was willing to risk what Walter Winchell called "a huge hunk of her own money" to portray Catherine the Great in the new drama *Empress of Destiny*. Rehearsals began February 4 under the direction of Ilia Motyleff, who had worked with Stanislavsky in Moscow. When it opened in March 1938 at Broadway's St. James, critics were merciless. On stage, Empress Catherine, with the aid of military leader (and lover) Potemkin, helps Russia become one of the great powers of Europe. Landi, on the other hand, dealt with what New York critic Richard Lockridge described as "a listless costume drama," and "was given nothing of real character to bite on." "It is hard to see how she can be blamed," Lockridge added. *New York Post* targeted the playwrights for a "barren ... dull ... inept" drama. The play closed after five performances.

<<>>

Was Elissa discouraged? No. She applied for her equity card in order to tour in summer stock. First up was *The Warrior's Husband*, which she performed at Cumberland Hills Playhouse (wearing Katharine Hepburn's original costumes). On May 10, 1938, she filed an amendment to her petition for naturalization.[210] Landi indicated that her permanent residence was an apartment at Central Park West. The following month she put her home in Pacific Palisades up for sale.[211] Sheilah Graham reported that Landi was asking $222,000. Graham said that Landi was determined to "divorce Hollywood 'completely'." Another year would pass before the The Cloisters sold, for which Landi ended up getting a total sum of ... *nothing*.

"Hollywood—I wasted seven good years of my life there"[212]
Elissa Landi

Happier days at The Cloisters. Niece Suki, Count Pi, Elissa, Bourban (horse), Tony, Annie, Westbound (horse), actress Kay English, Mildred McClure (Elissa's secretary)

DEERTREES THEATRE

HARRISON, MAINE

presents

ELISSA LANDI

in

"The Swan"

Between lectures and stage plays there were only 5 states in which Landi did *not* make a professional appearance

Chapter 11
On Tour & Down on the Farm

In the summer of 1938, Landi gained a reputation as the most traveled actress on the straw hat circuit. She frequently broke house records. After her revival of *The Warrior's Husband*, she headed to Long Island for the American premier of C.K. Munro's comedy *Veronica*. "Miss Landi really carried the play all by herself," raved one review. "She was admirably suited for the part." Landi revived *The Lady Has a Heart* for the grand opening of Washington D.C.'s Olney Theatre, an advance sellout. She then took the play, accompanied by Count Landi, to Cape Cod for the Playhouse's biggest week of the summer.[213] Her fondness for *The Lady Has a Heart*, buoyed by appreciative audiences, kept the play on her summer circuit for three years. Landi's preference for theater was rooted in her approach to playing characters. Being a writer tempered her feelings on the subject.

> A role cannot be created unless certain liberties are taken with the part. It is the duty of the actor to know all about the character. He should, at least mentally, write a complete biography of the character not only as he appears on the stage but also what sort of person he was as a child and during the time which may elapse in the progress of the play. In other words, the intention of the author must be clarified.[214]

<< >>

In mid-June, Elissa saw Nino off on the *Conte di Sevoia* with what was called a record-breaking hug. He was off to Verona to attend his sister's wedding. "7,000 Admirers Cheer as Film Star Kisses Martini," read one headline.

Seven thousand admirers shouted and screamed approval this noon as golden-haired Elissa Landi, actress, and his reported fiancée, kissed Nino Martini goodbye when he sailed for his home in Italy. After the Italian liner left the pier, the crowd turned its attention to the beauteous Elissa, who was waving farewell to her Nino. A flying squadron of ship line police rescued her from a thousand autograph seekers.[215]

All the ballyhoo prompted Walter Winchell to wag, "Elissa Landi says she isn't married to Nino Martini, which shows you how much *she* knows." Landi had written a syndicated news article titled, "This is Nino"—a charming and intimate look at the man she (obviously) cared about. In some ways, it was a reflection of herself.

We were throwing a rubber ball for my dog, Winkie, to run after. He caught it. I said to Nino, 'Winkie's a good mouser, too. Last night he caught a mouse.' 'Winkie catch a mou?' Nino's eyes were round. Much rounder than those of my niece, Sooky, aged 8. Sooky clapped her hands and laughed, 'A mou!' she repeated. And her adoration of Nino was more manifest than ever. He has religiously cancelled the ending consonants of almost every word he utters. The appeal of this is instantaneous. A mouse is a funny little creature, but a 'mou' is infinitely smaller, more endearing.

Landi then segues to a train trip with Nino across the U.S.

At night we would look at the moon and the moon drenched plains and he would sigh, 'Why don't people live in places like this? Why must they fight and kill and step on each other. The earth is so big, there is room for all.' Selfishness spoiled the good earth and made it ugly.

"Then New York," Landi continued. "Broadway for me [*The Lady Has a Heart*]."

> He used to collect me from the theater at night and we would walk along The Great White Way. Taxi drivers always called him by name. He would turn to me suddenly and say, 'I have a great desire sometimes, to have nothing at all, to be nobody. I want to be free and myself. I like forests and mountains and lakes and music. I like animals and children and the sun.' This he said, as he pushed his way through the mob on Broadway, being stopped every few steps by someone who recognized him ... They liked him, these people, so that pleased him. There was no pretense of being bored ... of being blasé. This is Nino. He isn't like anyone else.[216]

Nino's childlike spontaneity often turned heads. New York columnist Leonard Lyons observed Landi at the Stork Club trying to look nonchalant while Nino shot rubber bands at nude figures adorning the walls.

August 1937 - Elissa and Nino

<<>>

In October, Elissa began an extensive fall lecture tour at Wofford College in South Carolina. Her trek continued for months through a dozen states at various universities and community clubs. Lectures focused on: "The Difference Between Stage and Screen Acting." Her *modus operandi*? "I wander about, tell jokes and talk directly to people in the audience."[217] It was obvious she preferred the stage and was rather blunt about it. Audiences chortled as she acted the same scene (from *The Lady Has a Heart*) for the stage vs. the Hollywood camera, where an entire mood could be lost while beauticians tinkered with her face, or chased wild hairs a camera lens would magnify. "There is no audience but the camera," she would say. On stage, Landi pointed out, there was no chance of becoming the proverbial "face on the cutting room floor." "People often ask me," she mused, "if the movies can offer anything in the way of 'real art.' My reply to that is—'Ladies and gentlemen, I give you Mickey Mouse.'"[218]

Bolstering Landi's visibility (ironically) were screen revivals (by "popular demand," ads insisted) of *The Count of Monte Cristo* and *The Sign of the Cross*. Elissa would concede that on the plus side, motion pictures had tempered her tendency to overdramatize. "Before going [to Hollywood]," she said, "I had a tendency to be overly dramatic in my acting. You can't 'ham' on the screen—it's too obvious."[219]

During an interview with a high school reporter, Landi offered her fantasy for old age. "I want to get old and fat and rich and just write and write," she declared. "I do like writing better than acting. The greatest compliment one can pay me is to say, 'Miss Landi, I've never seen you act, but I've read such and such a novel of yours.'"[220] The ideal setting to get "old and fat and rich" would be a farm in Ulster county, just north of New York City. However, The Cloisters still hadn't found a buyer. One drawback that kept it on the market was the November fire that ravaged 14,000 acres in the hills of Santa Monica, destroying 600 homes. Flames came within two miles of Landi's residence.

It would take an automobile accident to allow Elissa respite from her hectic schedule. On December 17, driving over an ice-covered road in Ulster County, Landi's car skidded and crashed. She was thrown over the steering wheel and broke her collar bone. In the passenger seat was her step-father, who said that Elissa averted a worse accident by turning off the ignition.[221] Plans for a return to Broadway were put on hold. Despite injuries, the accident allowed her to put in many hours of writing. The crash, near the town of Kingston, would prove to be an uncanny location—for fate, fortune and the fulfillment of dreams.

<<>>

By February 1939, Landi was back on the lecture circuit. Her subject: film censorship. She blamed censors for "much of the deterioration" of Hollywood. Nino was frequently in the audience offering support, as he would be for her return to the stage in *Rebellion in Shadow. Rebellion ...* was an amusing look at a writer who falls in love with "the hero of her imagination." The premier took place at Maplewood Theatre in New Jersey. The playbill listed "Mady Francis" as the author, but days later Elissa revealed that *she* wrote the play. She didn't want anyone to think the story was autobiographical. ("Mady", of course, was her mother's nickname for Elissa when she was a child.) *Variety* noted, "Miss Landi has hit on a novel idea ... there's some scintillating dialogue. But the play falls short of Broadway requirements."

Landi then teamed with Orson Welles. "I think Orson Welles has stimulated the acting business a great deal," she said. "He represents the new trend of American theater."[222] The duo performed *Twentieth Century* for radio's Campbell Playhouse, produced by Welles. Landi played Lily Garland, a temperamental actress to Welles' veteran ham actor Oscar Jaffe (roles portrayed by Carole Lombard and John Barrymore in the 1934 film). Unfettered arguments between Welles' braggart Jaffe and Landi's tough, no-nonsense, Lily were the show's highlight.[223]

<<>>

Unwittingly, Elissa fulfilled her intention of finding the ideal residence and property—one that would allow her and Count Landi relaxation and ambition—they wanted to have their own dairy. It all happened "accidentally"—Landi explained:

> I was motoring to a lecture engagement in upstate New York when my car skidded and I was seriously injured. My collarbone was broken and my arm fractured. On the way to a local doctor we came upon a house for which I had been searching for so long—and I might never have found it if it hadn't been for two things—my career as a lecturer—and my accident.[224]

Closing documents for the Kingston property in the Catskill Mountains were signed in April. Landi took possession on May 1, 1939. The 123-acre estate, with fertile soil and woodlands, embraced an old fieldstone Colonial dwelling dating back to 1796. Another attraction was the nearby Woodstock art colony and Playhouse. A correspondent for *New York Evening Post* hastened to Kingston to get an inside scoop. While Count Landi, who loved "fixing" things, prepared to put up wood paneling over the living room's stone walls, Elissa took a break from scrubbing floors. "This is going to be home for father and me for the rest of our lives," she enthused. "And, we're going to farm the land. We're doing everything ourselves—no architect, no contractor. The furniture will be everything I've kept in storage ever since I gave up my house in Santa Monica." Landi had literally "given up" The Cloisters in Pacific Palisades—to the bank. In this way, she could manage to buy new property. Sheilah Graham reported another plus in Landi's favor: "Elissa Landi, former cinema favorite, gives lectures at the rate of 3 a week at $1,000 per gab and says, 'Even if I do no more film or stage work, I can still make $30,000 a year, and who wants more than that?'"[225]

Ulster County was not Elissa's first choice. "We looked in Connecticut for a house at first," said Landi, "but it was so neat and British we couldn't stand it. Everybody was such a damned lady or gentleman!"[226] Prior to her accident, Landi and the Count were leaning toward finding something in Ulster. She recalled, "As we approached this beautiful country up here, we noticed we kept getting gayer and gayer the further we came. I liked it, and I like it ever more now, for it isn't manicured ... it's really wonderful."[227]

<<>>

In July, Landi left Kingston to open the season for Stony Creek Playhouse in Connecticut. A young William Castle had just taken over the director's seat from Orson Welles (who had left for Hollywood to begin work on his script for *Citizen Kane*). Castle teamed with Landi for a revival of *The Lady Has a Heart*. Ironically, Castle's own legacy would include screen thrillers like *The House on Haunted Hill* and *The Tingler* starring Landi's former sensitive leading man Vincent Price. Following Landi's appearance at Stony Creek, Castle splattered swastikas on the playhouse. He claimed Nazis had done the deed, as he was starring a young German girl who had purportedly turned down an invitation to meet Hitler. Castle made news for this stunt, which (unsurprisingly) brought him a contract from Columbia Studios.

Landi didn't *need* any publicity shenanigans. *Boxoffice* reported, "Elissa Landi wowed them in *Lady Has a Heart* at Stony Creek one week and in *Tovarich* at Guilford Chapel Playhouse the next." From Connecticut, Landi arrived at Deertrees Theater in Maine for Ference Molnar's witty, romantic *The Swan*.

September 3, 1939. When England and France declared war on Germany, Elissa was starring at Woodstock Playhouse in another play she had written, *Holiday House*. The comedy-drama took place on Sunset Boulevard, and offered a behind-the-scenes look at a family tied to the film industry. The Playhouse was sold out. Hundreds were turned away. Landi's canine co-star was none other than her terrier "Winkie" who, instead of catching a "mou," took a bow and numerous curtain calls alongside his mistress. *Variety*, nonetheless, determined that Landi had "targeted Hollywood shallowness ... with a hodgepodge of unconvincing characters." Nino Martini was present ...

perhaps for the last time. From there afterward, little mention was made of the Landi-Martini combo. The couple had been an item for over three years.

Tenor Martini declared early on that he didn't get "engaged to people," and stuck to his word. But, at what cost? Landi's daughter Caroline told this author, "My mother had an abortion. She was heartbroken. The father was Nino Martini."[228] Landi, who had longed for a child, shattered by this turn of events, had only one consolation. Her relocation to the Kingston farm, which Elissa christened "Bright Acres," provided a much needed and healing distraction.

<<>>

In the Fall of 1939, The Cloisters found a buyer, Douglas Fairbanks Jr. Landi's former co-star, and his new wife Mary, opted to refurbish and modify the Spanish exterior before moving in. They rechristened their new home "Westridge." As mentioned, Elissa didn't get her asking price of $222,000. The bank had taken over, placing her estate on the market for what remained of the mortgage—$25,000. In his memoirs, Fairbanks wrote, "Apparently it had belonged to Elissa Landi, my leading lady from *The Amateur Gentleman*. I was told she was now virtually penniless. We decided then and there to nab it before anyone else ... it was wonderfully exciting, particularly as it was going to be so inexpensive."[229] (As of 2020, Steven Spielberg resides in "Westridge," which the director purchased from pop idol Bobby Vinton in 1986 for $7,500,000.")

Once the bank foreclosed on her home, Landi was forced to find other options. Plays and lectures allowed her the bankroll to purchase her farm, which she christened "Bright Acres." Fairbanks' comment about Landi being "penniless" was grounded in the fact that she quit making payments on the mortgage. And, as so often happens, gossip columnists fueled the "sad fate" stories of stars who abandon the film capital—especially one like Landi, who was accused of "rapping" Hollywood in her lectures. A clueless Hedda Hopper commented, "Fairbanks moved into his new home, which was practically a gift—price so low. Used to be the home of Elissa Landi. I wonder where she is and what she's doing?" Columnist Jimmie Fidler chimed in with, "No once-famous star ever dropped more completely from the limelight than Elissa Landi."

<<>>

Meanwhile in Los Angeles, brother Tony made news when publisher George Putnam, husband of the late Amelia Earhart, claimed to have received a life-threatening letter from a German sympathizer. It was typewritten in German, and Tony was credited as translating the letter. The missive demanded that Putnam suspend publication of *The Man Who Killed Hitler*.[230] Weeks later, Putnam declared to have been kidnapped, then bound and gagged in Bakersfield, before notifying police. Although Putnam denied it, this obvious hoax was geared to boost book sales. As *Time* magazine put it, "Publisher Putnam, who loves publicity, last week got plenty ... mystifying police with a tale of kidnapping by Nazis." (In 1914, Putnam had summed up *The Secret Life of an Empress* as "an abundant evidence of unreality.") Whether or not Putnam offered a cash bonus to Tony Landi for his services as "translator" remains a question to be answered. Tony was enlisted in the California State Guard, and employed as an insurance broker. He, wife Annie, and 9-year-old Sooky, resided at a home they had purchased on Napoli Drive in Pacific Palisades. In 1942 the couple would file naturalization papers.

Elissa, a naturalized citizen prior to the outbreak of war in Europe, also tackled the subject of subversive pro-Nazis in the U.S. From July-September 1940, she teamed with another Hollywood exile, actor Phillips Holmes, for the radio series, *Wings for America*. Landi traveled to Chicago for weekly broadcasts which focused on what was referred to as "the fifth column"—citizens who collaborate with national enemies. On air, Landi played a Chicago reporter, and Holmes a radio commentator. The stories were based on material released from police and government officials. Sadly, the good intentions of *Wings for America* were juxtaposed alongside U.S. government fears that German spies were infiltrating among Jewish refugees—resulting in the tightening of immigration restrictions. After the final episode, Landi took her patriotism a step further for the NBC program *I'm an American*. The series welcomed famous folks, as diverse as director Frank Capra and Albert Einstein, to explain why they became naturalized citizens. Elissa followed her own commentary by reading sketches she had written about immigrants. She was joined by William Marshall, the Assistant Director of the Immigration and Naturalization Service.

Landi lectures would evolve into exposing the torment of Jews in Germany. In June 1939, the U.S. had refused landing for a ship of Jewish refugees. 937 passengers were denied entry, forcing the ship to return to Europe where more than a quarter of them died in the Holocaust. For the opening of Washington D.C.'s Town Hall season (February 1941), Elissa offered the tragic scene of a Jewish refugee whose husband had been killed in a concentration camp. As the woman arrives by boat to American shores she cries, "Here one is still free; here people still smile; and here there are no secret police." Follow-up performances at various locations drew numerous curtain calls. One critic raved, "Nothing could mar the dramatic intensity of Miss Landi's performance."

<<>>

As far west as Salt Lake City, to New York's National Board of Review of Motion Pictures' annual conference, Landi received invitations to speak. Her opinions mattered. Along with extensive travels, planes, trains and hotels, came the accompanying stress. "I don't believe in nervous breakdowns," she said. "Let those who can afford them, have them. Often I get on the point of a breakdown, but I won't let myself have one."[231] Landi referred to herself as "de-married" and refused to answer questions about her private life, as well as her "relationship" with the late Empress Elisabeth of Austria. When she returned home to Kingston, Landi didn't slow down. Friends asked how she relaxed. Elissa replied, "By doing something else." "Something else" included showing up at New York's skyscraper nightclub, the Rainbow Room, wearing a blue velvet dress and winning first place in a waltz contest.[232] On the home front, Count Landi occupied his spare time by taking a correspondence course in agriculture from Cornell University.

Landi meets her fans

Spring of 1941. After a year-and-a-half absence from the stage, Landi returned in the romantic drama *Romance*, a 1913 play written by Edward Sheldon. Sheldon himself had selected Landi to play the prima donna (Garbo had done the film version). "Miss Elissa Landi got a real ovation in Kansas City for her *Romance* performance," reported Broadway critic Ward Morehouse. Landi was so taken with John Grogan, her young male lead, that she put him under contract. The duo performed in two more productions on the east coast: *The Lady Has a Heart* and *The Shining Hour*. One gossip monger let on, "Elissa describes John Grogan as 'my protégé,' but her intimates have a chummier word for it."[233]

There may have been some truth regarding the two "chums." During a Woodstock production of the romance *The Shining Hour*, a reporter interviewed Landi. At the very mention of Grogan, Elissa grew "terribly enthusiastic." The duo were planning to do *Romeo and Juliet*.[234] Instead of Shakespeare, Landi-Grogan ended up reviving their previous success, *Romance*. *Buffalo Evening News* thought Landi "bewitching" and Grogan did "well enough" in a "quaint, perfumed souvenir of the pre-World War theater."

By the time sister-in-law Annie and niece Suki arrived at Bright Acres, Elissa's romantic notions had turned quite serious .... and *not* with Grogan. In 2020, Suki remembered, "At the time we stayed with her, Elissa was in the throes of an affair with Clifton Fadiman. My mother told me Elissa wanted him to divorce his wife and marry her, but he told her his wife was Catholic and didn't believe in divorce."[235] Gossip columnists somehow hadn't detected the Landi-Fadiman affair. Fadiman, a noted intellectual and writer, was in charge of the book review section of the *New Yorker*, and moderator for radio's popular quiz show *Information Please!* True (and lasting) romance for Elissa, however, would have to wait another year.

Another romance at Bright Acres involved a sow and a boar. "My aunt's Kingston farm," recalled Suki, "had two pigs, a male and female called Adolph and Unity." Unity Mitford was a British socialite who championed Nazism and was obsessed with Führer Hitler. Humor at Bright Acres, was supplemented with heart. Elissa's housekeeper, Faithful Truth, an African-American, was a follower of Father Divine, a charismatic, controversial (and wealthy) African-American spiritual leader, who championed racial equality. "Faithful once took me to his sumptuous estate," said Suki, "where she stayed when on vacation." Suki especially liked Faithful's roasted turkey and stuffing, with cranberry jelly. Suki always referred to Elissa as "Mamou" - a term of endearment. Elissa's nickname for Annie was "Nicky." She obviously had great affection for her sister-in-law and niece ... and the man who made it all possible. The dedication page for Landi's next book was inscribed, "To Tony - with love."

<<>>

Women and Peter **dedicated to brother Tony**

Landi's book *Women and Peter* was written while at Bright Acres. Released in October 1941, the contemporary love story had a theatrical background. Protagonist Peter is a New York playwright. His own personal drama involved a youthful affair with his best friend's stepmother. Years later, the woman's daughter fosters another emotional upset (and affair) for Peter. One critique compared Landi's style to F. Scott Fitzgerald: "Seldom since the days of Fitzgerald have a group of characters been so acutely aware and analytical of themselves." Landi admitted, "*Women and Peter* was based on incidents and characters that I knew well. I don't think that it's possible to write fiction that is entirely unrelated to personal experience."[236] A critic for

179

London's *The Stage* noted, "The people of the theatre who figure in it are well known and the whole story is thoroughly readable."

Landi indicated that, due to the war, successful plays had to either reflect the headlines, or provide a complete escape from reality. One vehicle Landi added to her repertoire in 1942, was purely escapist fare: *Theatre* (based on the Somerset Maugham novel). The comedy opened at New York's Flatbush Theatre, before heading to Cambridge. Elissa relished the role of Julia Lambert, a respected veteran English actress—so good, in fact, that she never stops acting. Doubts about aging and sex appeal push Lambert to flirt with a younger man in hopes to quash her surmounting fears. *Boston Herald* applauded, "Miss Landi's work was of the caliber we have come to expect of this fine actress." Elissa revived *Theatre* frequently over the next several years.

In August, Landi was at Toronto's Royal Alexandra Theatre. *Variety* reported that her performance in *Romance* could have been held over for a second week, but Gloria Swanson was contracted for a play. After Swanson's final bow, Landi was asked to return for the lead in Maxwell Anderson's *Mary of Scotland*.

<<>>

As 1942 came to a close, Elissa Landi, "film star," found herself in Hollywood making what some designated as a "comeback." Unbeknownst to her, earlier that year, she had met her future husband.

Chapter 12
"I Think We're Shining, Don't You?"

December 7, 1942. A year after the bombing of Pearl Harbor, Elissa arrived on the set of *Corregidor*. The film focused on the Japanese campaign that overtook Manila Bay. Landi was assigned the role of a surgeon. "Here was an opportunity," she said, "to depict the part one woman played in the hell of that defense of the Philippines ... and to bring home to others, as it had to me, the difficulties and hardships which countless unsung heroines are facing. I knew right then and there that I had a job to do ... that would have its own unique importance in the war effort."[237] The action took place in jungles, fox holes, and the island fortress of Corregidor, prior to the surrender in May 1942, of 11,000 American and Filipino troops.

A love triangle emerges while bombs blast the Philippines. Landi and husband Otto Kruger, a bacteriologist, arrive at Corregidor, where they are joined by Landi's former lover, Donald Woods, also in the medical field. Although she is in denial, Kruger senses that Landi still has feelings for Woods. During an air raid, Kruger dies. As emergency rations are depleted, Landi and the nurses who work in underground caverns, are ordered to evacuate. Woods and Landi vow to reconnect after the war. He stays behind taking care of the wounded. At the finish we see Landi shedding tears—not knowing the fate of Woods, or if he will ever return.

The script had been approved by the War Department. William Nigh, known for his prolific output of "B movies," signed on as director. On December 3, trade journals announced that Landi had the female lead. Following her five-year hiatus from the screen, the two-week shoot sped by quickly. The film was shot by PRC (Producers Releasing Corp.), one of the less prestigious, low-budget, studios. *Corregidor* was touted as their most ambitious feature to date. One added plus for Elissa, was having her niece Suki visit the set.

Louella Parsons got on the bandwagon welcoming Landi back. "Elissa Landi who might have been another Greer Garson with the right breaks, will return to pick up her movie career. I think the intelligent, well-read Landi was ahead of her time." A poverty-row studio wasn't exactly the "right break" to make a comeback (which was not Landi's intention). *Corregidor* wasn't in the same league as *A Farewell to Arms*. Even so, *Photoplay* made a point of saying, "Miss Landi is very good in her role and should be seen more often." A New York critic admired Landi's performance, saying, "It is good to see Miss Landi back on the screen. She takes the melodramatics of *Corregidor* gracefully in her stride, and, as always, comports herself with intelligence."[238]

Some critics used caution. After all, the film was a tribute to the men and women in the armed forces. *Syracuse Herald* felt that the combat scenes "added considerable punch to this super-quickie. The film is chiefly held together by the performances." *Variety* went on a scathing rant. "*Corregidor* is a feeble picture that does no credit to its subject. Its unmotivated, undeveloped, ineptly written, clumsily produced and directed ... inexcusably played." Repetitious use of aerial stock footage posed a problem for the analytic viewer, but the film had its merits.

While *Corregidor* lacked the polish of a major studio and a top-notch script, the cast worked in ensemble, not trying to outshine each other, but to tell a human story. Landi, Kruger, and Woods, whose character was burdened with his own insecurities, offer a genuine display of emotion, sensitively done.

Corregidor (1943) Landi and Donald Woods (PRC)

183

As the love-triangle unravel their feelings, we are offered an occasional dash of humor, and see the effect of prolonged combat upon one soldier on the verge of shell-shock. While the film registers as propaganda, it avoids the stereotypical caricatures of Japanese that were prevalent at the time. The film also casts a skeptical eye on traditional male-female roles. Aside from technical defects and uneven musical score, *Corregidor* is worth watching. It has balance. The love themes and military conflicts interweave smoothly upon what the patriotic epilogue designates as "the blood red rock, Corregidor."

<<>>

Without taking a break, Landi prepared for her nightclub debut (December 23) at the Casbah, one of New York's plusher venues. Elsa Maxwell, Peggy Wood, Gertrude Lawrence, Moss Hart, and Oscar Hammerstein were among those attending opening night. Columnist Earl Wilson imbibed at the Casbah that evening, then toasted, "What magnificence, what cover charge! And in our fevered minds that unforgettable picture—of Elissa Landi oozing across the floor in a $30,000 fur coat (it wasn't hers). Making her first nightclub appearance, Miss Landi ... did two sketches, one of a group of would-be actresses in a tryout, another of a woman who came to call on her, and apparently learn English. They got a very nice applause." Afterward, Wilson asked Landi why nightclubs? "I thought it would be fun," she replied. "For a long time I've been doing rather serious things."[239]

The day after she closed at the Casbah (January 5), Elissa got serious again. For radio's popular *Suspense!* she begged co-star George Coulouris to help out her fiancé, convicted of robbery. Coulouris, it appears, knows too much. Landi's carefully drawn emotions and befuddled determination were just the ticket to build "suspense." Landi then appeared in a stage revue titled "Women Can Take It!"—a benefit for the Citizen's Committee for the Army and Navy. For this, she impersonated the late Amelia Earhart. Rivoli Theatre hosted the event, prior to screening the world premier of Hitchcock's *Shadow of a Doubt*. In mid-February, it was announced that Landi was returning to

Broadway. When asked about her role, she answered, "I suppose you could call me a Greek chorus of one. But really, this kind of part poses a whole new set of problems for the actor." Apparently, she knew what she was getting into.

APOLOGY

THE PLAYBILL

Apology (1943) with Erin O'Brien-Moore and Thelma Schnee

Apology, produced and directed by Lee Strasberg, opened March 22 at the Mansfield. Strasberg was co-founder of Group Theater and proponent of method acting. He cast Landi (first billed) as "The Lecturer"—a shadowy figure who introduces scenes and utters sagacious commentary. The play itself focused on a relentless tycoon with no scruples—destined to become a lonely, solitary figure. *New York Times* opined, "Miss Landi has a mountainous task which probably no one could fully accomplish." In his private journal, Tennessee Williams, there for opening night, jotted down, "Just came from seeing Elissa Landi in an incredibly bad play."[240] A Boston critic said of Landi, "her interpretations and comments—beautifully spoken always—accomplish no good purpose and destroy any continuity of action." Critic Louis Kronenberger berated playwright Charles Schnee as being "all too 'literary' without knowing really how to write." The play's verbosity and structure was the problem. Drama critic John Ferris summed up, "The play was bad; the actors good." *Variety* confirmed that *Apology* was "a screwy idea." It closed after eight performances. Schnee had better luck as a screenwriter with the classic Hollywood exposé, *The Bad and the Beautiful* (1952)—for which he received an Oscar.

<<>>

After the demise of *Apology*, did Elissa give up on Broadway? No. Did she take a break from touring? Absolutely not. As her African-American housekeeper Faith, told one reporter, "I've worked for actresses all my life but that Miss Landi—she won't stay in bed!"[241] Faith knew of what she spoke, having been with Elissa and the Count for over three years. Reporter Ray Peacock substantiated Faith's comment: "If you were to make a list of the world's busiest women, Elissa Landi's name would be right near the top. For here is a young woman who simultaneously pursues four careers, and makes them all pay."[242] Fact was, there were only five states in the union in which Landi had *not* made a professional appearance. She kept a map of the U.S. with pins indicating location after location. Aside from actress, lecturer, and author, Peacock included "farmer." Fifty of Landi's acres in the Catskills were under cultivation. "I've got a cow and a Victory Garden and a flock of chickens," she enthused. As a consequence, the government supplied her with four income tax forms.

Columnists indicated that Landi was thinking of running for State Senator in the next election (1946). Her intentions would focus on a post-war farm education platform.[243] Per request from the Ulster County Publicity Committee, Landi began appearing on metropolitan radio broadcasts to boost the county's visibility as an ideal vacation destination. Other radio gigs included co-starring with Ray Milland in the rowdy *This Thing Called Love*, as newlyweds who opt to put their marriage on trial and not to sleep together. The Legion of Decency had condemned the film version. In the summer of

1943, amid a whirlwind of plays, lectures, and entertaining wounded soldiers at Ft. Devens, Elissa found time to get married. The romance began on May 5, following a Boston performance of Shaw's *Candida*.

Elissa Landi, in her own words:

> Shortly after the curtain fell on our final scene, there was a knock on my dressing room door, and I opened it to a very tall, dark-haired young man, whose hat seemed strangely familiar. "I know this hat and this man—" I told myself, "but from where?" I came up with, "Mr. Curtis, how nice." "Curtis Thomas," he corrected me with a smile. "Remember—Cambridge, cocktails, and our literary agent?"

The light dawned and Landi invited him in. Curtis asked if she were free that evening, but Elissa had scheduled a date with a Marine. After fifteen minutes, she rose up and put on her hat. "Either there has been a misunderstanding, or I'm being stood up."

> "Is it my pleasure to take you to supper?" Curtis asked. I remember thinking that the old-fashioned phrase sounded most refreshing. I have learned since that he has a certain inherent formality that is very endearing—and never, never stuffy. We spent the evening drinking coffee and talking. Everything under the sun came up for discussion; in fact, we were so absorbed in our conversation that the time flew and we found ourselves practically thrown out of the restaurant at three in the morning. Still talking, we walked back to the Ritz, where I was staying. I had never enjoyed anyone's company so much. "Landi," I sent myself a mental note, "You're hooked." Little did I realize that only a few months later ... a broken date, would evolve into a ring around my third finger, left hand, after an exciting summer romance.[244]

Elissa and Curtis first met in June 1942. She was starring in *Theatre* at the time. Her literary agent came backstage to discuss Landi's novel, *The Pear Tree*. She made mention of her client Curtis Thomas, who had written a historical novel. Days later, Elissa crossed paths with a young man wearing what she described as "a battered and beloved-looking felt hat." He immediately identified himself. "By the way, Miss Landi. We have a mutual friend. My literary agent." "*You* are the man," she replied, "who wrote the historical novel!" They chatted briefly over cocktails, before she rushed off to the theater. As Elissa put it, "It wasn't until I was lucky enough to get stood up by my Marine Captain—eleven months later—that we really got to know each other."

Curtis and Elissa were "lucky enough" to have one dinner date before *Candida* closed. He wrote her regularly. "His letters," she described, "had the same warmth, understanding and absorbing interest as his company. I was suddenly set back on my heels by a lovely sonnet for me which he had enclosed in a letter ... I began to look forward to those verses. And they became more romantic and more charming with each letter." During a return engagement to Boston, Curtis and Elissa continued to "click." She invited him and two other guests to Kingston. When they arrived, Count Landi informed her that housekeeper Faith had up and left! Father Divine had relocated to Philadelphia. Elissa detailed,

> It was then that Curtis displayed another talent. He came to the rescue with a burst of domesticity that was amazing. One day, he and I were weeding the beet patch. I was talking about my plans for the immediate future. "I'm going to arrange my life so I can just stay on the farm," I told him, frowning at a weed, "and write." "Just write?" "Well," I considered, "I expect to do a radio program soon." "Where," he asked without looking at me, "do I fit into these plans?" "What?" I looked at him quickly. "You know I'm madly in love with you," he said gently. I dissolved into tears. It wasn't until that moment when he looked so earnestly in my

eyes and told me he loved me that I realized how important he was in my life.

Matrimony - August 28, 1943

Elissa and Curtis were married inside the Gothic architecture of Christ Church on Park Avenue, August 28, 1943. Immediate family and four close friends were on hand to offer support and good wishes. "All the fun in life is doubled, as if by magic," declared Elissa, "when there is another person to share it."

<<>>

Curtis Kinney Thomas - Harvard, Class of 1926

Curtis Kinney Thomas was born September 1, 1905 in Cortland, New York. He was an alumni of Harvard University, Class of 1926. As a member of the Glee Club, he sang with the Boston Symphony at Carnegie Hall. After graduation he traveled to France, England, Bermuda, the British West Indies and resided for awhile in Morocco. In early 1934, Curtis ventured to Hollywood where he reportedly spent a few months engaged in writing and scenario work for films.[245] He occasionally wrote articles for the *Cortland Standard*, and magazines such as *Adventure* (1934). Later on, his stories appeared in such popular venues as *McCall's* and *Esquire*. In 1934, Curtis' *Allegro-Piano Quartet in G* was performed at local recitals. At the time of his marriage, Curtis was teaching at the Harris school in Chicago.

After two days of wedded bliss, Elissa was back at it. From her apartment in Manhattan, leased just prior to marrying Curtis, she headed to Pittsburgh for the feminine lead in the Chicago company of *Tomorrow the World*. The play had created a sensation on Broadway, running 500 performances. Landi and cast, opened September 13 at the Nixon Theater—husband Curtis, in tow. *Variety* reported, "Show went over big with Nixon first-nighters and should be a winner on tour." It was. Elissa was engaged in *Tomorrow the World* for twenty-nine weeks.

On stage, an adolescent German orphan (Dickie Tyler) is transplanted to a small university town in the Midwest. His uncle (Paul McGrath), a broadminded professor, believes he is rescuing the boy, whose father had been tortured and killed by Nazis. The boy's mind, however, has been warped, indoctrinated beyond repair. He is bent on breaking his uncle's engagement to a Jewish school teacher (Landi), and attempts to take the life of his small cousin. The school teacher, despite her experience as a child psychologist, is baffled as to what steps to take. The play posed the dilemma of a post-war world coping with Hitler-trained youth. Across the board, critics found the play to be an absorbing experience.

Tomorrow the World 1943-44 (Selwyn Theatre, Chicago)

After Pittsburgh came Detroit, Cleveland, Columbus, Milwaukee, and finally Chicago, where *Tomorrow the World* ran for 19 weeks at the Selwyn Theater. The play sustained itself with commanding performances. A critic for the *Columbus Dispatch* felt that Landi and McGrath gave "surprising substance to vaguely written roles." Eleven-year-old Dickie Tyler offered an "extraordinary piece of acting." The youngster had a natural grasp of the role's implications. *Chicago Daily Times* thought Landi and McGrath were "first-rate all the way," and called Tyler "a pint-sized marvel" who, after doses of unrelenting kindness, collapses in sobs at the play's end.

Off-stage, Landi kept busy. She supported her friend Orson Welles' Free World Movement, which championed the creation of a United Nations. The organization would soon become a target of the notorious House Un-American Activities Committee. At Christmas, Elissa appeared at the Volunteers of America headquarters to help distribute food baskets to needy children. A reporter for *Chicago Daily News* watched youngsters focus on Elissa, who gently reminded them, "Let us not forget the men in battle who have given up safety and comfort ... let us not forget to be grateful for what we have that so many in Europe have lost."

Husband Curtis was always nearby. He was engaged to teach seven youngsters, five who were in the cast of *Tomorrow the World*. Curtis jokingly referred to them as "stage brats." "I am tutoring the lot of them three afternoons a week and liking it enormously. They happen to be first-rate individuals ... how they carry this particular production has to be seen to be believed."[246] The kids occasionally put him on the spot. He admitted, "I am not prepared to hear myself quoted verbatim two days after I have let slip some half-baked remark that has been whipped up from the ingredients of a faulty memory." Elissa helped tutor Latin. Curtis confided, "My wife and I do not react automatically to the patter of little feet—when we hear them neither of us reaches for the nearest box of candy ... we just look suspicious." It's no wonder that Elissa enjoyed her husband's company. On a very personal level, Mr. and Mrs. Thomas would soon be put to the test in regard to "the patter of little feet." Two weeks before *Tomorrow the World* left Chicago, Landi left the cast. It was April 2 ... and she was five months pregnant.

<<>>

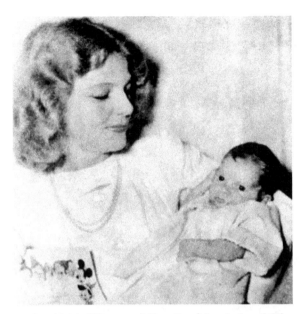

September 1944 - Elissa and Caroline Maude Landi Thomas

On September 10, 1944, Caroline Maude Landi Thomas made her world debut at Woman's Hospital in New York City. At long last, Elissa's dream of motherhood had arrived. She and Curtis awarded their daughter with a Walt Disney Certificate War Bond, during the "Buy a Bond for Baby Campaign." It would hang on her nursery-room wall. Caroline was also blessed with a young godfather, twelve-year-old Dickie Tyler, the Nazi brat from *Tomorrow the World*. Tyler wrote Louella Parsons that he was "very proud" of his new role. (By 1960, Tyler was highly respected in the field of bodybuilding. When his friend Arnold Schwarzenegger became governor, Tyler was appointed to the California State Chiropractic Board).

One month into motherhood, Elissa signed with producer Sam Grisman for the lead role in *Dark Hammock*. Rehearsals began in mid-October. Tryouts were held in Philadelphia, Boston, and Washington D.C. The story dealt with an ex-showgirl's attempt to poison her elderly husband, in order to claim his Florida estate. Enter Dr. Florence McDavid (Landi) and her assistant Amelia (Mary Wickes), who are in the area researching exotic wildlife. The quick-

193

witted doctor suspects what is going on, and tricks the Mrs. into swallowing the final lethal dose meant for the husband.

DARK HAMMOCK
A NEW PLAY
By MARY ORR and REGINALD DENHAM

with
ELISSA LANDI
MARY WICKES   CHARLES McCLELLAND

Fall 1944 - *Dark Hammock*

Philadelphia Inquirer found the "sustained mounting tension" to be "richly rewarding." "Miss Landi," the review indicated, "Is vital and capital as the alert, intelligent doctor." *Boston Herald* complimented the "vivid characterizations." Opening December 11, at Broadway's Forrest Theatre, the play crashed after two performances—the record short-run of the season. *New York Post* found the plot implausible. *New York Sun* felt that the authors had "not bothered to give their characters the breath of life." Critic Arthur Pollock was more moderate in his opinion. "Elissa Landi does her prying charmingly" in what he described as "a leisurely thriller." *Dark Hammock* would be Elissa Landi's final bow on Broadway.

<<>>

Elissa's Mercia in *Sign of the Cross* made a comeback in 1944. DeMille added a prologue set in WWII, with planes flying over ancient Rome. Conversation between soldiers onboard segues to the original film's opening scene. Elissa told one reporter that she could still recall the sonorous "Jehovah-like quality" of Cecil B.'s voice. "It was one of those days where everything was going wrong," she said. DeMille began threatening extras to be quiet. One extra paid no mind. DeMille demanded to know who it was, and what they had said. A bedraggled Roman citizen volunteered, "I *said*, that I wished the big so-and-so would dismiss us for lunch." DeMille positioned his microphone, and shouted, "Lunch!"[247]

Elissa's co-star in *The Sign of the Cross*, Fredric March, starred in the December 1944 release of *Tomorrow the World*. Skip Homier reigned-in the role of the belligerent German youth, stealing the show. March admitted, "My part ... isn't outstanding—the picture really belongs to the boy—but I wanted to be in it for what it has to say."[248]

<<>>

Landi was always welcomed by enthusiastic audiences in Toronto, where she spent January-February 1945 starring in such classics as *Candida*, *Romance*, and *Berkeley Square*. She was also reunited with Alexander Kirkland in *Blithe Spirit*. It had been a dozen years since the two had co-starred at Fox. They were a huge success at the Royal Alexandra. *Blithe Spirit* was held over for a second week. In March, Elissa took *Candida* to Montreal, where she also did a broadcast for the French version of Lux Radio. She then headed home for multiple broadcasts as moderator for Mutual Radio's *Between Us Girls*. "Curtis is my best critic," said Elissa. "He and Caroline Maude stay home and listen to me every Wednesday night. Like everything else I do these days it's fun because happiness makes the whole world seem wonderful."

The combination of motherhood and tours was fun, but strenuous. During a June run of *Blithe Spirit* in Cambridge, Curtis and Caroline Maude resided with his parents in Newburyport, two hours north. Elissa explained,

My present system is to get up early enough in the morning to get the baby's breakfast, and catch the 8:30 train to Boston. Then we rehearse all day and in the afternoon I try to get a train that will take me home about the time the baby is finishing her supper, which Curtis has prepared. And in the evening there's her laundry and other little items, dishes to wash—anyone can fill up the blanks. Next week I'll have to reverse my schedule; stay at Cambridge at night and spend the days in Newburyport.

Blithe Spirit broke a six-year box-office record. At Cape Playhouse, Landi tried out *This Was a Woman*, a recent London success written by Joan Morgan. In this psycho-shocker, Landi played a bored housewife and birdwatcher, who evolves into a power-hungry murderess.

Elissa's major priority at this juncture, was reserved for daughter Caroline. Elissa carried a wallet full of photos and needed no nudging to show them off.

Caroline Maude was born last September, and naturally I think she's very pretty. She's very gay and happy, and from five months showed exceptional interest in music, rocking herself in time to little songs that I sang to her. As the first grandchild on either side of the family, she is quite an event, but she won't be an only child, as I'd like to have two more.[249]

March 1945 marked the release of Elissa Landi's final novel *The Pear Tree* (copyright 1944). By Christmas, it was in its third printing, along with French and Italian versions. In Landi's stream-of-consciousness style, the narrative begins when a famous American female poet unexpectedly dies. Mona, a close friend, tries to unravel the mystery. D.C.'s *Evening Star* surmised, "The merit of this novel lies in its clever manipulation of material ... it is carried out with ingenuity. The manner in which Elissa Landi brings the truth to light ... is well-calculated drama." Mona is an intriguing presence. She has native Choctaw roots and enjoys swimming naked in the moonlight ... wondering

196

about the mysteries of nature and life. Mona carries a torch for a musician who often waxes metaphysical. During one mellow interlude he asks her, "I think we're shining, don't you?"

> *Sometimes I think our bodies are just lamps. On certain days the lamps are cloudy and then the light inside is only faintly visible. Then our eyes are dull and our fellow men pass us by. But sometimes we're clear, cleaned and polished by perception, and then even a casual bystander notices the light. And his heart is lifted—although he himself may not know why.*[250]

The Pear Tree

October 1945 - Radio's *Powder Box Theater* with Jim Ameche

After several radio appearances, Landi teamed with Conrad Nagel in a fall revival of *Tomorrow the World*. She then took a long break to spend Winter and Spring with young Caroline.

<<>>

1946 allowed Elissa respite from a hectic schedule. She spent time at home mothering her young toddler, enjoying husband Curtis, and her old standby Count "Pi" Landi. In May, she returned briefly to radio (CBS) to read excerpts from *The Pear Tree*. In July she revived John Van Druten's nostalgic comedy *The Damask Cheek* at Woodstock Playhouse. Elissa played the niece of a very proper Victorian aunt. A local critic commented that Landi was the only cast member who stayed in character, but that her "reactions could be taken at a quicker pace." A critic from Saugerties countered, "Miss Landi delineates the part with a finesse that wins for her a hearty round of applause."

A six month sabbatical from the stage found the actress taking ... her own sweet time. A week later, Landi lent some spark as Elvira in Noel Coward's *Blithe Spirit* at Saratoga's Spa Theater.

A Dream Come True: Elissa and daughter Caroline

When she arrived in Saratoga, Elissa found the cast unprepared, and took over as director. One review praised, "She whipped up a comparative miracle in three days ... to present the best performance of the season." In August, Landi took Shaw's *Candida* to Cape May, then back to Woodstock. Opening night, the house was filled to capacity. Landi crowned her thespian skill that fall, on NBC radio's "The Playhouse of Favorites" in Henrik Ibsen's *The Doll's House*.

During the post-war surge of television entertainment, Landi was asked to join the staff at City College of New York (January 1947). This Tuesday evening position focused on elocution and speech, and encouraging new talent. Touted as the school's "most glamorous instructor," Elissa zeroed in on the main problem students were up against: a lack of general education. She also indicated that Americans had a problem with men who took interest in culture, labeling them effeminate, instead of respecting their abilities.[251]

In June, Landi began a summer circuit of plays that included Shaw's *Pygmalion*. Eliza Doolittle proved to be an ideal role for Elissa, and was an unqualified hit with Woodstock audiences. A critic mentioned the "brilliance" and "perfection" of the production, the many curtain calls and enthusiastic applause. One audience member, however, *wasn't* so thrilled. In 2004, daughter Caroline recalled,

> When I was two, I went to see her in George Bernard Shaw's *Pygmalion*, and at the beginning of the play a man knocks flowers out of her hand. At that point, I let out a shriek. I had to be taken out of the theater. I don't remember this, but my father told me the story many times. He always loved it.[252]

Landi closed the summer season in *The Barretts of Wimpole Street*. As the invalid poetess Elizabeth Barrett Browning, she was praised as being "sure and appealing in her role." Elissa then opted for more controversial material. She guest-starred on WNEW radio's "Lest We Forget-The American Dream"—a series dealing with problems of prejudice and discrimination. In the episode *Occupation Housewife*, Landi turns a local woman's club topsy-turvy by championing membership for a foreign-born applicant.

In the fall, husband Curtis saw the release of his novel *Devil Take the Foremost* (Doubleday). It was selected by the Crime Club to be on their honor roll. One critic noted the ability of the author to get "tentacles into the reader's mind." And, as 1947 came to a close, The Lions Club of Kingston honored Elissa Landi as their "Woman of the Year." She was now on the faculty of Kingston's Academy of St. Ursula, where she taught English and diction. Her devotion and championing of the community meant a great deal to local residents.

1948

Television. In late 1945, Elissa starred in the first hour-long narrative TV show telecast from Manhattan. In January 1948, her appearances on NBC's "Author Meets the Critics" were simultaneously broadcast on TV and radio. On March 18, the guest author was Landi's former co-star Adolphe Menjou. Menjou's autobiography *It Took Nine Tailors* was critiqued by Landi and film producer Jesse L. Lasky. Discussions on this series could be quite heated. Elissa and husband Curtis were inspired to produce their own TV series—a husband-and-wife breakfast talk show.[253] General Electric surveyed their home in Kingston and town house apartment in New York, to begin the installation of electronic transmitters. Health issues intervened.

Dr. Kenneth Lefever, Landi's physician, diagnosed in early 1948 that she had abdominal cancer. He informed Curtis of his decision *not* to reveal the negative prognosis to Elissa, as it could impede recovery. An operation for a cancerous tumor followed.[254] At the time, it was common practice to keep cancer diagnoses secret from the patient. Many felt it would spare them anguish. In Elissa's case, she bounced back while working on her seventh novel. She and Curtis also co-wrote a play titled *After Aurora Sings*, which she intended to take on the summer circuit.

In August, Landi returned to Woodstock Playhouse for another revival of Maugham's witty, *Theatre*. She then signed with WNEW (New York) for its upcoming 13-week radio series, "How to Speak Better English." *Variety* indicated that there was a throng of auditions from those wanting to get "the Pygmalion treatment from Miss Landi." On September 18, an enthusiastic audience greeted Elissa for the revue *Don't Worry Mac* ... a benefit for the Woodstock Playhouse. For this, she offered a "most amusing interpretation of six young women auditioning to be the ingénue in a Theater Guild production." Famed cartoonist Rube Goldberg emceed the event. Adding to Landi's visibility that Fall was another reissue of *The Count of Monte Cristo*.

In October, Landi was all set to begin a lecture circuit at Winthrop College in South Carolina. Her cancellation on October 7, was due to what was described as "a chronic condition." She was replaced by Alexandra Tolstoy, daughter of Leo Tolstoy, author of *War and Peace*. Elissa entered Kingston Hospital where, for several days, she kept slipping into a state of unconsciousness. The cancer had spread to her brain. A week later, she rallied sufficiently to communicate with her family. Brother Tony, now an associate producer, had arrived from Los Angeles. Two days later paralysis struck— her condition, "critical." At 4 a.m. on October 21, Landi passed away. Her husband was at her bedside. Dr. Lefever praised Curtis for the manner in which he was able to handle the situation.

On October 22, the Kingston funeral home of A. Carr & Son welcomed over a hundred friends and professional associates for a viewing. The funeral service, however, was private.[255] The following June, Bright Acres had an estate sale. Five percent of the proceeds were designated, by Curtis Thomas, for the Chicago Tumor Institute. His intention was to provide funds for cancer research. A fine collection of Oriental rugs, French tapestry and 17th-18th-19th century antiques, were in the offing. The $20,000 estate would go to four-year-old Caroline, who had relocated with her father to Massachusetts.[256]

Caroline spent the rest of her childhood with her grandparents, Fred and Maude Thomas, on Rings Island at the northeastern tip of Massachusetts. When I spoke to Caroline in the summer of 2020, she was plain-spoken and direct. "My mother did not want me to be raised by my grandparents. There was a great deal of contention between my father and his mother. My father was gay. This did not please his mother. There was a feeling of disconnect between the two. Truth had to be hidden, and there was a great deal of sorrow."[257] Curtis found respite from the situation when he was hired as a college professor in New Jersey. He visited daughter Caroline every other weekend. Needless to say, it was a difficult atmosphere to grow up in.

Losing her mother at a tender age had lasting consequences for Caroline. When she saw her mother for the last time, Elissa, prior to her stay at the hospital, had slipped into unconsciousness. "There was a door that connected my bedroom to my parents' room," recalled Caroline. "I was determined to get through that door so I could see my mother. My father was physically restraining me. No child should ever see anyone, let alone their mother, in the last stages of brain cancer. I went into a panic. I began screaming and left the room. My father followed me and gave me a spanking." Curtis was obviously at a loss of how to handle such a situation. Nonetheless, Caroline emphasized what a gentle, loving presence he was while she was growing up. In the aftermath, Caroline's memories of Elissa are minimal.

> On the one hand, I got to know her from the point of view of a very young child. So my remembered mother is all bits and pieces that others help me to fit together. Of course, I had my father's memories - but he, also, knew her for a short time. There was so much of her life that he heard about, but hadn't actually experienced with her.[258]

It took decades before Caroline realized a personal breakthrough in regards to the loss of her mother. In 2017, she detailed,

> I didn't mourn her consciously - I think this happens when you're 4. You just put it down into the unconscious. It's all there, but you don't remember it. Then I got cancer six years ago, the same illness she had, and when I came out of that I realized my mother did not abandon me. And I understood many things about problems I've had in my life. I've always thought people would leave. So I would put them at arm's length so I would have control, so they just wouldn't disappear. I do remember my mother now a little bit, after six years of intensive work, mostly through teaching and writing - I've written over 100 poems and several stories, in which I appear using the name of one of my mother's most famous movie characters. She was an extraordinary woman and her legacy has followed me a great deal.[259]

<< >>

After Elissa had reached the proverbial final curtain, theater critic Hal Eaton wrote in his column, "Broadway mourns the passing of the brilliant Elissa Landi. A talented actress, playwright and novelist, she was a warm and understanding human being." Landi's legacy is "still shining" in many respects ... encapsulated in the visual art of film, the audio world of radio, the library of written words ... and surely in the unknown spheres that she hinted at in her novel, *The Pear Tree*. Elissa recognized the ability to step out of time and thought - to experience the perpetual presence and wonder of simply ... being.

Sometimes I would steal out at night and swim naked. The water was warm and it felt good to be alone and awake in a sleeping world. I would float and consider the mystery of the night, wondering whether this deep hour had the same effect on animals as on mankind. And often I contemplated my existence and asked myself what we were all doing ...

Sometimes I think our bodies are just lamps. On certain days the lamps are cloudy and then the light inside is only faintly visible ... But sometimes we're clear, cleaned and polished by perception, and then even a casual bystander notices the light. And his heart is lifted ...

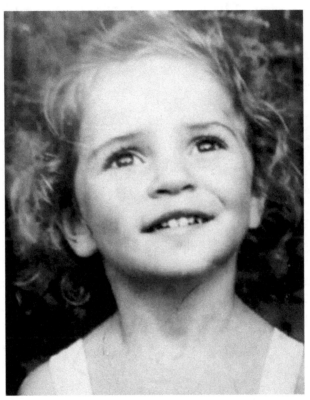

1948 - "… and the heart is lifted" - Caroline age four, shortly before her mother passed away.

Afterword

In the aftermath of his stepdaughter's death, Count "Pi" Landi returned to Los Angeles to live with Tony in Pacific Palisades. Elissa's niece Suki remembers Pi as "short, fair-skinned and blue-eyed. He lived with us on Napoli Drive. He suffered from what was then called *senile*." The Count filed his naturalization papers (June 1949), and received his U.S. Citizenship on April 25, 1952. Pi died on August 2, 1953. News items ballyhooed his claim to being the last English resident convicted of piracy. "Last of Britain's Pirates is Dead," read headlines in both England and the U.S. Apparently, this 1924 caper was his proudest achievement. Charles "Pi" Zanardi-Landi was 77 years old.

Count Pi - naturalization photo (1949)

By 1948, brother Tony had left behind his career with Lloyd's of London to become an associate producer (as Anthony Z. Landi) for Orbit Productions. Films included: *Parole Inc.* (1948) starring Michael O'Shea, and *Alimony* (1949). In the summer of 1949 it was reported that Tony was busy prepping a film version based on Elissa's *The Pear Tree*.[260] Sadly, the film wasn't made. Tony was also associate producer for Gloria Film Productions' *Three Husbands* (1950), and *The Scarf* (1951) with John Ireland and Mercedes McCambridge. Throughout the rest of his career, Tony was involved with several companies in the U.S., Germany, and England, producing films, television programs, and commercials.

By 1958, Tony had returned to England to live permanently. He and his wife Annie resided at Eaton Place, one of the luxury areas in London's Belgravia district. He was listed in the government's *London Gazette* as a "motion picture financier." Daughter Suki noted, "I know my parents were friendly with Elissa's first husband John Lawrence when they returned to the U.K." (Lawrence died in 1973). Annie passed away in February 1963. In April 1964, Anthony married Jane Golden Lester, ex-wife of his best friend, and relocated to the St. Marylebone district. Their son Christopher was born in September 1964. When Anthony passed away on December 29, 1975, he was 73 years old.[261]

**Elisabeth "Suki" Landi Sennett - 1947 graduation photo,
University High School, Los Angeles**

Tony's daughter Suki was impressed with her aunt Elissa's inherent intellectualism. She felt that Elissa had missed her true calling. "Elissa would have had a happier life if she had been able to go to Cambridge like my father," she told this author. "Instead, she ended up supporting the family."[262] The role of "Professor Landi," according to Suki, would have better suited Elissa's innate talents. It wasn't until her final two years that Elissa tackled this role at New York City College. Suki herself received a Master's Degree in Theater Arts at UCLA. She was then hired for a position at San Jose State College, where she taught modern dance, and stage movement for the drama department.

In 1955, Suki married Al Sennett, a San Francisco lawyer. The couple resided in Sausalito. In 1982, she completed the Women's Public Affairs Internship Program at Coro Fellowship in San Francisco. For the next 20 years Suki served as an analyst for Marin County. She was honored in 2005 for her service as Commissioner on The Frank Lloyd Wright Conservancy (a State and National Landmark). As of 2020, Suki still resides in Sausalito, where she is involved with The League of Women Voters.

When I asked Suki Landi Sennett about her connection to the Hapsburg dynasty, and *The Secret of an Empress*, she admitted, "I never discussed the book with my parents." Her grandmother Caroline's claims, as Elissa herself demonstrated, belonged to the distant past. Even so, Suki related that when she ventured to Vienna a couple of years ago, she purchased souvenirs bearing the name "Sisi" (nickname for the Empress). When Suki returned home to California, she gave them to her friends. "We all got a big laugh out of it," she chuckled.

When the subject of Curtis Thomas came up, Suki was matter-of-fact. "Something happened between my father and Curtis. There was a falling out."

<<>>

In June 1951, columnist Ed Sullivan reported that Curtis Thomas was studying for the priesthood. Instead of the ministry, Curtis stuck with teaching, lecturing, and writing. After daughter Caroline completed her sophomore year at Barnard College (Manhattan), she and her father ventured to Europe (late summer of 1964), and lived there for five years. She took the opportunity to visit her uncle Tony, and meet her mother's first husband John Lawrence.[263] While in London, Caroline attended the Royal Academy of Dramatic Art. From there, she headed to New York to pursue an acting career. In 2002, Curtis died in New York at the age of 97. He was interred at Oak Hill Cemetery in Newburyport, Mass. Oak Hill is also the final resting place for Elissa and her mother Caroline.

Oak Hill Cemetery, Massachusetts

Caroline credits her father Curtis for making her life "very interesting." "He just took me around," she stated. "He knew all kinds of people; he was interested in everybody. I was a fly on the wall - I picked up everything just by watching."[264] During the 1970's Caroline kept busy with acting assignments Off-Broadway. It was her mother's legacy that prompted her towards an acting career. Caroline admitted, "I didn't enjoy acting. I was shy." As the years went by, Caroline gravitated toward *teaching* dramatic arts. She was casting director for the film *Anna* (1987),which earned Sally Kirkland an Academy Award nomination.

Daughter Caroline, after completing three years at London's Royal Academy of Dramatic Art. More recently, as founder of Total Theatre Lab

Caroline found lasting happiness with her third husband Robert L. Benes. The couple met briefly at an acting class in 1974, and rekindled their relationship ten years later. They married in 1989. Caroline and husband Robert created Total Theatre Lab in Manhattan, which has been operating for the last 30 years. Recently, Caroline assisted French actress/writer Nelly Alard with the novel *La Vie Que Tu t'Etais Imaginee* (2020) (*The Life You've Imagined*). The possible connection between Elissa Landi and the House of Hapsburg is at the crux of this mystery novel, which *Elle* magazine called, "A gripping investigation shot through with cheerful humor."

The Landi Legacy

In 1976, author James Robert Parish penned *Hollywood Players- The Thirties*, which included an overview of the life and career of Elissa Landi. Parish set the precedent for numerous other film tomes that paid tribute to Landi. He confirmed that it was Elissa's role in *The Sign of the Cross* that "would be her most memorable screen appearance and would insure her place in the Thirties' cinema."[265] As previously mentioned, Parish proposed that in *The Count of Monte Cristo*, Landi "offered her finest screen performance." In conclusion, Parish said of Landi, "there were a few sparks of glory throughout her career," and that she remains "a large mystery in the annals of royal lineage."

The visibility of Elissa Landi continues through numerous film revivals at venues such as the Museum of Modern Art in New York, and the British Film Institute in London. Since 1994, Turner Classic Movies has screened numerous films from Landi's career, thus creating a steady fan base for her unique gifts and talent.

The legacy of Elissa Landi is confirmed by a star on the Hollywood Walk of Fame. She was inducted on February 8, 1960. The Elissa Landi star is located at 1611 Vine Street (West side), near the Ricardo Montalban Theatre. The town of Kingston, New York, had honored Landi as "Woman of the Year" in 1947, and subsequently named one of their county roads: Elissa Landi Drive (though misspelled "Elisa"). This tribute curves along Catskill Park and through the wooded countryside, with scenic views that reflect Elissa's love of nature.

< < > >

Landi lent both grace and subtlety to the screen. She offered dramatic weight, not for show, but only to flesh out her characters. Elissa was adamant that she not be pigeonholed by the Hollywood studio system into being a "star" - a persona she would have to play off-screen as well as on. This made Landi unique, and one can only respect her decision, her courage, and her willingness to face the consequences. In spite of the many problems she faced, her connection to writing, music, and mother earth, allowed Elissa Landi perspective and, on occasion, the ability to live in the moment, to take pleasure in contemplating ... the moon.

Acknowledgements

I was fortunate to have onboard for this venture into the life and career of Elissa Landi, my regular band of troupers. Author James Robert Parish provided me with various rare Landi film titles. As mentioned, his 1976 volume *Hollywood Players - The Thirties* (currently available in both paperback and Kindle), offers an excellent overview of Landi's life, including her film career in England and Hollywood.

My good friends Jenny Paxson and Larry Smith, both associated with film preservation for the Library of Congress, were generous with their input and materials from their private collections. Their work on behalf of the Library of Congress Packard campus in Arlington, Virginia, is impressive. The duo invited me twice to introduce films at the Packard Campus Theater film festival, a true highlight in this author's career. Jenny is a devoted fan of Elissa's co-star from *The Amateur Gentleman* (1936), Doug Fairbanks Jr. She does an excellent job with detailing Fairbanks Jr.'s career (with rare memorabilia) on Facebook.

Graceann Macleod, a talented writer in her own right, provided her astute insight and expertise as a proofreader for the sixth time. We began our association while I was working on *Ann Harding - Cinema's Gallant Lady* (2010). Graceann and her husband David live in London. Be sure and check out David Macleod's *The Sound of Buster Keaton* (1995), soon to be reissued on Kindle.

2017-Larry Smith and Jenny Paxson joined Joel and Scott for lunch in Warrenton, Virginia

Graceann Macleod displays a beautiful cross stitch item she helped create for the International Buster Keaton Society Auction (2003)

Film aficionados Fedo Coke, Eric Monder, Andrew Wentink, film critic/columnist David Noh, and author Joseph Egan also provided source material and ideas for the Landi biography. In 2018, when I mentioned my Landi project, Egan told me, "There is a hell of a story there and one I have been wondering about for years. What the hell happened? I mean, who did she piss off?"[266] Egan tackled the controversial child custody trials of Mary Astor in his acclaimed 2016 book, *The Purple Diaries* (Diversion Books).

I had been contemplating writing about Elissa for a few years, and began the project in late 2017. In 2016, writer and critic for *Classic Images*, Laura Wagner, asked me, "Have you ever considered writing about Elissa Landi? I am currently researching Landi for a profile for my encyclopedia and she just struck me as someone you would do."[267] When I ran the idea of a Landi biography by my publisher Ben Ohmart, he readily agreed that the time was right, and that Elissa deserved having her story told.

I had the good fortune to get the support of Elissa's daughter Caroline Landi Thomas, and Elissa's niece Suki Landi Sennett. Family, of course, is the life's blood of any biography. Especially when they share with honest spontaneity, and are candid in their assessments. I appreciate Caroline and Suki's willingness to participate during the rather chaotic, pandemic summer of 2020 - a time which Caroline aptly described as being "very hard to think straight." Caroline's heart and humor are genuine, as reflected in the Introduction she wrote for this biography.

My husband Joel Bellagio provided the computer and technical skills for archiving the films and memorabilia that help fuel the Landi narrative (including a Skype session with her daughter Caroline). He watched Elissa's films with keen interest, and was always forthright with his opinions. Joel's penchant leans towards character actors such as Louise Fazenda, Frank McHugh, Aline MacMahon, Guy Kibbee, and the Stanislavsky-trained Maria Ouspenskaya. On the stellar-side, he connects with Norma Shearer, Alice Faye and Dick Powell. Needless to say, Joel boosts my confidence, making the process feel like a real cosmic adventure.

Tomorrow the World (1943-44)

Credits

STAGE
1924:

Dandy Dick (Oxford Repertory Theatre) by Arthur Wing Pinero; D: J. B. Fagan; Cast: Athene Seyler, Glen Byam Shaw, Elissa Landi (Sheba), Reginald Smith, Alan Napier

Everybody's Husband (Oxford Repertory Theatre) by Gilbert Cannan; D: J.B. Fagan; Cast: Elissa Landi (A Girl)

Storm (Ambassadors) by C.K. Munro; Cast: Elissa Landi (Storm), Alan Napier, Hugh Wakefield, Jean Cadell

1925:

The Painted Swan (Everyman) by Elizabeth Bibesco; Cast: Elissa Landi (Selina), Edith Evans, Robert Harris, Frank Cellier, Felix Aylmer, Allan Jeayes

Kismet (New Oxford) by Edward Knoblock; Cast: Sam Livesey, Elissa Landi (Marsinah), Benita Hume, Mary Clare, Robert Harris, Herbert Grimwood

Lavender Ladies (Comedy Theater) by Daisy Fisher; Cast: Herbert Marshall, Louise Hampton, Mary Jerrold, Elissa Landi (April), James Raglan, Jean Cadell

1926:

Blind Alley (Playhouse) by Dorothy Brandon; Cast: Sam Livesey, Ion Swinley, Elissa Landi (Gloria)

Benediction (Everyman) by G.M. Carlyon and G.M. Burlton; Cast: Elissa Landi (Ursula), Austin Trevor, Stanley Lathbury, Raymond Massey

Punch and Go (Everyman) by John Galsworthy; Cast: Elissa Landi (Venessa), Edmund Willard, Norman Page, Nancy Price

217

The Constant Nymph (New Theatre) by Margaret Kennedy and Basil Dean; D: Basil Dean; Cast: Noel Coward, Edna Best, Basil Dean, John Gielgud, Elissa Landi (Antonia), Cathleen Nesbitt

1927:
Othello (Lyceum) by Shakespeare; D: A.E. Filmer; Cast: Robert Loraine, Ion Swinley, Elissa Landi (Desdemona), John Gielgud, Alan Napier, Ernest Thesiger
Glimpse of Reality (Arts Theatre) by George Bernard Shaw; Cast: Elissa Landi (Giulia), Terence O'Brien, Harcourt Williams

1929:
The Stag (Globe Theatre) by Beverley Nichols; D: Raymond Massey; Cast: Elissa Landi (Marion), Ian Hunter, Reginald Owen, Martin Sands
After All (Apollo Theatre) by John van Druten; D: Auriol Lee; Cast: Richard Bird, Elissa Landi (Greta), Helen Haye, Una O'Connor, Cyril Raymond, Frederick Lloyd, Norah Balfour, Muriel Aked

1930:
After All (Arts Theatre) by John van Druten; D: Auriol Lee; Cast: Laurence Olivier, Elissa Landi (Phyl), Helen Haye, Cathleen Nesbitt, H.G. Stoker, Muriel Aked
A Farewell to Arms (National Theatre) by Laurence Stallings (based on the Ernest Hemingway novel); D: Rouben Mamoulian; Cast: Glenn Anders, Elissa Landi (Catherine), Harold Huber, Jack La Rue, Crane Wilbur

1935:
Tapestry in Gray (Shubert Theatre) by Martin Flavin; D: Marion Gering; Cast: Elissa Landi (Iris), Melvyn Douglas, Minor Watson, Dick Van Patten, Arnold Korff

1937:
The Lady Has a Heart (Longacre) by Ladislaus Bush-Fekete; D: Rufus Phillips: Cast: Vincent Price, Elissa Landi (Countess Katinka), Hilda Spong, Judith Alden, Lumsden Hare

1938:
Empress of Destiny (St. James) by Jessica Lee and Joseph Lee Walsh; D: Ilya Motyleff; Cast: Elissa Landi (Catherine), Glenn Hunter, Helen Raymond, Robert Payson, Dennis Hoey
The Warrior's Husband (on tour); by Julian F. Thompson; Cast: Elissa Landi (Antiope)

Veronica (on tour); by C.K. Munro; Cast: Elissa Landi (Veronica), Dennis Hoey, Albert Tarbell

The Lady Has a Heart (on tour); by Ladislaus Bush-Fekete; Cast: Elissa Landi (Countess Katinka), Hilda Spong, Arnold Korff, Leslie Dennison

1939:

Rebellion in Shadow (on tour) by Elissa Landi (pseudonym Mady Francis); Cast: Elissa Landi

The Lady Has a Heart (on tour) by Ladislaus Bush-Fekete; Cast: Elissa Landi (Countess Katinka)

Tovarich (on tour) by Jacques Deval (adapted by Robert E. Sherwood); D: Hardie Albright; Cast: Elissa Landi (Tatiana)

The Swan (Deertrees Theatre, Maine) by Ferenc Molnar; D: Bela Blau Cast: Elissa Landi (Alexandra), Hilda Spong

Holiday House (on tour) by Elissa Landi; Cast: Elissa Landi (Isabel), Paul Hammond, Winkie

1941:

Romance (on tour) by Edward Sheldon; Cast: Elissa Landi (Rita Cavallini), Jack Grogan

The Shining Hour (on tour) by Keith Winter; D: Robert Elwyn; Cast: Elissa Landi (Olivia Riley), Jack Grogan, Karl Malden

The Lady Has a Heart (on tour) by Ladislaus Bush-Fekete; Cast: Elissa Landi (Countess Katinka), Jack Grogan

Another Language (on tour) by Rose Franken; Cast: Elissa Landi (Stella)

1942:

Theatre (on tour) by Guy Bolton (from the novel by W. Somerset Maugham); Cast: Elissa Landi (Julia Lambert)

Romance (on tour) by Edward Sheldon; Cast: Elissa Landi (Rita Cavallini), Jack Grogan, Lloyd Bochner, Arthur Jarret

Mary of Scotland (on tour) by Maxwell Anderson; D: Frank McCoy; Cast: Elissa Landi, William Harrigan

1943:

Apology (Mansfield Theatre) by Charles Schnee; D: Lee Strasberg; Cast: Elissa Landi (The Lecturer), Erin O'Brien-Moore, Theodore Newton, Harold J. Stone

Candida (on tour) by George Bernard Shaw; Cast: Elissa Landi (Candida), Jack Grogan

The Damask Cheek (on tour) by John Van Druten; Cast: Elissa Landi (Rhoda)

Theatre (on tour) by Guy Bolton (from the novel by W. Somerset Maugham); Cast: Elissa Landi (Julia Lambert), Jack Grogan

Tomorrow The World (on tour through April 1944) by James Gow and Arnold d'Usseau; D: Elliott Nugent; Cast: Elissa Landi (Leona), Paul McGrath, Dickie Tyler, Joan Shepard, Russell Collins

1944:

Dark Hammock (on tour; Forrest Theatre) by Mary Orr and Reginald Denham; D: Reginald Denham; Cast: Elissa Landi (Florence McDavid), Mary Wickes, Charles McClelland, Arthur Hunnicutt, Scott Moore

1945:

Blithe Spirit (on tour) by Noel Coward; Cast: Elissa Landi (Elvira), Alexander Kirkland, Vicki Cummings

Candida (on tour) by George Bernard Shaw; Cast: Elissa Landi (Candida)

Romance (on tour) by Edward Sheldon; Cast: Elissa Landi (Rita Cavallini), Alexander Kirkland

Berkeley Square (on tour) by John Balderston (based on the Henry James novel *The Sense of the Past*); Cast: Elissa Landi (Helen Pettigrew), Bramwell Fletcher

This Was a Woman (on tour) by Joan Morgan; Cast: Elissa Landi (Olivia)

Tomorrow the World (on tour) by James Gow and Arnold d'Usseau; Cast: Elissa Landi (Leona), Conrad Nagel

1946:

The Damask Cheek (on tour) by John Van Druten; Cast: Elissa Landi (Rhoda), Edith King

Blithe Spirit (Spa Theater) by Noel Coward; D: Elissa Landi; Cast: Elissa Landi (Elvira), Kate Harrington

Candida (on tour) by George Bernard Shaw; Cast: Elissa Landi (Candida)

1947:

Theatre (on tour) by Guy Bolton (from the novel by W. Somerset Maugham); Cast: Elissa Landi (Julia Lambert), Richard Kendrick

Pygmalion (Woodstock Playhouse) by George Bernard Shaw; Cast: Elissa Landi (Eliza Doolittle), Cort Steen, Francis Bavier

The Shining Hour (on tour) by Keith Winter; Cast: Elissa Landi (Olivia Riley), Karl Malden

The Barretts of Wimpole Street (on tour) by Rudolf Besier; Cast: Elissa Landi (Elizabeth Barrett), Cort Steen, Roland Hogue, Francis Bavier

1948:
Theatre (Woodstock Playhouse) by Guy Bolton (from the novel by W. Somerset Maugham); Cast: Elissa Landi (Julia Lambert)
Don't Worry, Mac (Woodstock Playhouse) a revue; D: Clarence J. McCarthy; Cast: Elissa Landi, Rube Goldberg, Ham Fisher

Wicked (1931)

After the Thin Man (1936) Elissa with James Stewart (MGM)

FILM (by release date)
1926:
London British National Pictures (October) D: Herbert Wilcox; Cast: Dorothy Gish, John Manners, Hubert Carter, Gibb McLaughlin, Margaret Yarde, Elissa Landi (Alice Cranston), Daisy Campbell, Adelqui Millar, Paul Whiteman

1928:
Underground British Instructional Films (BIF) (July) D: Anthony Asquith; Cast: Elissa Landi (Nell), Brian Aherne, Norah Baring, Cyril McLaglen
Bolibar British Instructional Films (BIF) (July) D: Walter Summers; Cast: Elissa Landi (Francoise-Marie /La Monita), Michael Hogan, Hubert Carter, Carl Harbord, Jerrold Robertshaw, Cecil Barry, Evelyn Roberts
Synd (Sin) British Instructional Films (BIF) (September) D: Gustaf Molander; Cast: Lars Hanson, Elissa Landi (Jeanne), Anita Hugo, Gina Manes, Hugo Bjorne, Stina Berg

1929:
The Inseparables Whitehall Films (March) D: Adelqui Millar, John Stafford; Cast: Elissa Landi (Velda), Pat Aherne, Annette Benson, Gabriel Gabrio, Jerrold Robertshaw, Fred Rains

1930:
Knowing Men United Artists (February) D: Elinor Glyn; Cast: Elissa Landi (Korah), Carl Brisson, Jeanne de Casalis, Helen Haye
The Parisian Pathe-Natan (French version May 1930 English version August 1931) D: Jean de Limur; Cast: Adolphe Menjou, Elissa Landi (Yvonne), Roger Treville, Charles Redgie, Olga Valery
The Price of Things United Artists (July) D: Elinor Glyn; Cast: Elissa Landi (Anthea), Stewart Rome, Walter Tennyson, Mona Goya, Dino Galvani, Marjorie Loring
Children of Chance British International Pictures (November) D: Alexandre Esway; Cast: Elissa Landi (Binnie/Lia), Mabel Poulton, John Stuart, Dorothy Minto, John Longden, Kay Hammond, Wallace Lupino

1931:
Body and Soul Fox (February) D: Alfred Santell; Cast: Charles Farrell, Elissa Landi (Carla), Humphrey Bogart, Myrna Loy, Don Dillaway
Always Goodbye Fox (May) D: Kenneth MacKenna and William Cameron Menzies; Cast: Elissa Landi (Lila), Lewis Stone, Paul Cavanagh, John Garrick, Frederick Kerr, Lumsden Hare, Herbert Bunston, Mischa Auer, Mary Gordon

Wicked Fox (October) D: Allan Dwan; Cast: Elissa Landi (Margot), Victor McLaglen, Una Merkel, Irene Rich, Alan Dinehart, Theodore von Eltz, Mae Busch, Ruth Donnelly, Edith Fellows, Jacquie Lyn Dufton

The Yellow Ticket Fox (October) D: Raoul Walsh; Cast: Elissa Landi (Marya), Lionel Barrymore, Laurence Olivier, Walter Byron, Arnold Korff, Mischa Auer, Edwin Maxwell, Rita La Roy, Gilbert Emery, Boris Karloff, Henry Kolker, Sarah Padden

1932:

Devil's Lottery Fox (March) D: Sam Taylor; Cast: Elissa Landi (Evelyn), Victor McLaglen, Alexander Kirkland, Ralph Morgan, Paul Cavanagh, Barbara Weeks, Beryl Mercer, Herbert Mundin, Halliwell Hobbes, Lumsden Hare, Alan Dinehart, Mary Gordon, Ethel Griffes, Dennis O'Keefe

The Woman in Room 13 Fox (May) D: Henry King; Cast: Elissa Landi (Laura), Ralph Bellamy, Neil Hamilton, Myrna Loy, Gilbert Roland, Walter Walker, Luis Alberni, Charlie Grapewin

A Passport to Hell Fox (August) D: Frank Lloyd; Cast: Elissa Landi (Myra), Paul Lukas, Warner Oland, Alexander Kirkland, Donald Crisp, Earle Foxe, Yola d'Avril, Herman Bing

The Sign of the Cross Paramount (December) D: Cecil B. DeMille; Cast: Fredric March, Elissa Landi (Mercia), Claudette Colbert, Charles Laughton, Ian Keith, Arthur Hohl, Harry Beresford, Tommy Conlon, Ferdinand Gottschalk, Vivian Tobin, Joyzelle Joyner, Nat Pendleton, George Bruggeman, Charles Middleton, Mischa Auer, John Carradine

1933:

The Warrior's Husband Fox (April) D: Walter Lang; Cast: Elissa Landi (Antiope), Marjorie Rambeau, Ernest Truex, David Manners, Helen Ware, Maude Eburne, Ferdinand Gottschalk, John Sheehan, Lionel Bellmore, "Tiny" Sanford

I Loved You Wednesday Fox (June) D: Henry King and William Cameron Menzies; Cast: Warner Baxter, Elissa Landi (Vicki), Victor Jory, Miriam Jordan, Laura Hope Crews, June Lang, Mischa Auer, George Bruggeman, Charles R. Moore

The Masquerader Samuel Goldwyn (UA) (September) D: Richard Wallace; Cast: Ronald Colman, Elissa Landi (Eve), Juliette Compton, David Torrence, Claude King, Halliwell Hobbes, Helen Jerome Eddy, Bill Elliott, Creighton Hale

By Candlelight Universal (December) D: James Whale; Cast: Elissa Landi (Marie), Paul Lukas, Nils Asther, Dorothy Revier, Lawrence Grant, Esther Ralston, Warburton Gamble, Lois January, Luis Alberni, Paul Porcasi

1934:

Man of Two Worlds RKO (January) D: J. Walter Ruben; Cast: Francis Lederer, Elissa Landi (Joan), Henry Stephenson, J. Farrell MacDonald, Walter Byron, Forrester Harvey, Ivan F. Simpson, Lumsden Hare, Christian Rub, Steffi Duna, Sarah Padden

Sisters Under the Skin Columbia (April) D: David Burton; Cast: Elissa Landi (Judy), Frank Morgan, Joseph Schildkraut, Doris Lloyd, Clara Blandick, Shirley Grey, Samuel S. Hinds, Henry Kolker, Selmer Jackson

The Great Flirtation Paramount (June) D: Ralph Murphy; Cast: Elissa Landi (Zita), Adolphe Menjou, David Manners, Lynne Overman, Raymond Walburn, Adrian Rosley, Paul Porcasi

The Count of Monte Cristo United Artists (September) D: Rowland V. Lee; Cast: Robert Donat, Elissa Landi (Mercedes), Louis Calhern, Sidney Blackmer, Raymond Walburn, O.P. Heggie, Irene Hervey, Georgia Caine, Luis Alberni, Douglas Walton, Juliette Compton, Clarence Wilson, Clarence Muse, Leon Ames

1935:

Enter Madame Paramount (January) D: Elloitt Nugent; Cast: Elissa Landi (Lisa Della Robia), Cary Grant, Lynne Overman, Sharon Lynn, Frank Albertson, Cecilia Parker, Michelette Burani, Paul Porcasi, Diana Lewis, Richard Bonelli, Ann Sheridan, Matt McHugh

Without Regret Paramount (September) D: Harold Young: Cast: Elissa Landi (Jennifer), Paul Cavanagh, Frances Drake, Kent Taylor, Gilbert Emery, David Niven

Koenigsmark (*Crimson Dynasty*) Capital Film Corporation (October) D: Maurice Tourneur; Cast: Elissa Landi (Princess Aurore), John Lodge, Pierre Fresnay, Frank Vosper, Allan Jeayes, Romilly Lunge, Marcelle Rogez

1936:

The Amateur Gentleman Criterion (April) D: Thornton Freeland; Cast: Douglas Fairbanks Jr., Elissa Landi (Lady Cleone Meredith), Gordon Harker, Basil Sydney, Hugh Williams, Irene Browne, Athole Stewart, Coral Browne, Margaret Lockwood, Esme Percy, Frank Bertram

Mad Holiday MGM (November) D: George B. Seitz; Cast: Edmund Lowe, Elissa Landi (Peter Dean), ZaSu Pitts, Ted Healy, Edmund Gwenn, Edgar Kennedy, Soo Yung, Charles Trowbridge, Rafaela Ottiano

After the Thin Man MGM (December) D: W.S. Van Dyke; Cast: William Powell, Myrna Loy, James Stewart, Elissa Landi (Selma), Joseph Calleia, Jessie Ralph, Alan Marshal, Teddy Hart, Sam Levene, Penny Singleton, Charles Trowbridge, George Zucco, Paul Fix, Asta

1937:

Hollywood Party MGM short (April) D: Roy Rowland; Cast: Elissa Landi (hostess), Charley Chase, Leon Errol, Joe Morrison, The Jones Boys, Clark Gable, Joan Bennett, Freddie Bartholomew, Joe E. Brown, Anna May Wong, Betty Jane Rhodes

The 13th Chair MGM (May) D: George B. Seitz; Cast: Dame May Whitty, Madge Evans, Lewis Stone, Elissa Landi (Helen), Thomas Beck, Henry Daniell, Janet Beecher, Ralph Forbes, Holmes Herbert, Heather Thatcher, Charles Trowbridge, Robert Coote, Lal Chand Mehra

1943:

Corregidor PRC (March) D: William Nigh; Cast: Otto Kruger, Elissa Landi (Dr. Royce Lee Stockman), Donald Woods, Frank Jenks, Rick Vallin, Wanda McKay, Ian Keith, Ted Hecht, Ruby Dandridge

Documentary Shorts

Screen Snapshots - Series 15, No. 5 Columbia (January 1936) 10 minutes D: Ralph Staub; Cast: Vince Barnett, Mary Brian, Bruce Cabot, Eddie Cantor, Elissa Landi, Dick Powell, Eddie Quillan, Gene Raymond, Raquel Torres, Warren William

Screen Snapshots - Series 16, No. 1 Columbia (September 1936) 10 mintues D: Ralph Staub; Cast: Virginia Bruce, James Cagney, Lily Damita, Bette Davis, Madge Evans, Errol Flynn, Betty Furness, Ann Harding, Elissa Landi, Marian Marsh, Ken Maynard, Frank McHugh, Cesar Romero, Rosalind Russell, Ann Sothern, Johnny Weissmuller

So You Think You Know Music No. 2 Columbia (March 1942) 10 minutes Cast: Elissa Landi, Hendrik Willem Van Loon

June 21, 1937 - Lux Radio presentation of *Monsieur Beaucaire* with host Cecil B. DeMille. Elissa and co-star Leslie Howard

RADIO
1926:
The White Chateau (London broadcast: August 16) by Reginald Berkeley; Cast: Elissa Landi (Diane), Reginald Denham, Gordon McLeod, Henry Oscar

1933:
Shell Show (CBS - October 16) Pete Smith (MC), Guests: Elissa Landi, Alice Brady, Frank Morgan, Nelson Eddy
The Troubadours (NBC - November 29) Guest: Elissa Landi

1934:
Hollywood on the Air (NBC - July 29) Elissa Landi interviewed by columnist Jack Grant

1935:
Shell Chateau Show (NBC - April 20) Al Jolson (host) Guests: Elissa Landi, Benay Venuta
Lux Radio Theater (NBC - May 26) *Michael and Mary* starring Elissa Landi (Mary Rowe), Kenneth MacKenna
Rudy Vallee Show (NBC - July 25) Guest: Elissa Landi
Lux Radio Theater (NBC - December 2) *The Swan* starring Elissa Landi (Princess Alexandra), Alfred Shirley

1936:
Shell Chateau Show (NBC - February 29) Al Jolson (host) Guests: Elissa Landi (in a dramatic sketch), Una Merkel
Camel Caravan (CBS - August 11) Rupert Hughes (MC); *By Candlelight* starring Elissa Landi (Marie), Otto Kruger; Benny Goodman band, Nathaniel Schilkret orchestra
Kraft Music Hall (NBC - October 22) Bing Crosby interviews Elissa Landi and Cary Grant
Lux Radio Theater (NBC - December 7) Host: Cecil B. DeMille presents *Grand Duchess and the Waiter*; Cast: Elissa Landi (Grand Duchess Xenia), Robert Montgomery, Alma Kruger
Lessons in Hollywood (NBC) Host: Jackie Cooper; Guest: Elissa Landi

1937:
Kraft Music Hall (NBC - May 13) Bing Crosby (host); Guests: Elissa Landi, Lionel Stander, Josephine Tumminia, John McCormack, Jimmy Dorsey orchestra

Lux Radio Theater (NBC - June 21) Host: Cecil B. DeMille presents
Monsieur Beaucaire; Cast: Leslie Howard, Elissa Landi (Lady Mary
Carlisle), Pedro De Cordoba

Shakespeare Cycle (CBS - August 16) *As You Like It*; Cast: Elissa Landi,
Dennis King, Gail Patrick, Moroni Olsen, Frank Morgan

Sunday Night Party (NBC - August 22) Host: James Melton; Guest: Elissa
Landi

Magic Key of RCA (NBC - October 31) Milton Cross (MC) Guests:
Elissa Landi and Vincent Price enact a scene from *The Lady Has a Heart*, Jan
Kiepura (tenor)

1938:

Hammerstein's Music Hall (CBS - March 18) Guests: Elissa Landi,
Fredda Gibson, George Bertran

The Monday Night Show (CBS - May 16) Guests: Elissa Landi, Connie
Boswell, Richard Himber Orchestra

Tommy Riggs and Betty Lou (NBC - November 26) Guest: Elissa Landi

1939:

The Campbell Playhouse (CBS - March 24) *Twentieth Century* (by Charles
Bruce Millholland); Cast: Orson Welles, Elissa Landi (Lily Garland), Sam
Levene, Ray Collins, Everett Sloane

Gotham Nights (WOR - July 2) Guests: Elissa Landi, Bramwell Fletcher,
Maxine Sullivan (vocalist)

1940:

Fifth Row Center (Mutual - March 31) *The Secret Glory* starring Elissa
Landi

So You Think You Know Music! (CBS - April 28) Guest: Elissa Landi

Fun in Print (CBS - June 16) Guests: Sinclair Lewis, Elissa Landi,
Genevieve Taggard

Fifth Row Center (Mutual - June 21) *Enemies Within* starring Elissa Landi,
Phillips Holmes

Wings for America (Mutual - 10 weeks - July 5- September 6) Starring:
Elissa Landi (Lorna Carroll), Phillips Holmes

1941:

We Hereby Resolve (Mutual - January 1) Guests: Elissa Landi, Paul Lukas,
Konrad Bercovici

Your Happy Birthday (WJZ - Baltimore - January 3) Guests: Elissa Landi,
Ralph Forbes, Jill Esmond, Jimmy Dorsey's Orchestra

I'm an American (NBC - February 16) Guest: Elissa Landi

Lincoln Highway (NBC - April 12) Guest: Elissa Landi, Sterling Holloway

Colonel Stoopnagle (CBS - May 27) Guests: Elissa Landi, Monty Wooley, Patty Berg

Armstrong's Theatre of Today (CBS - October 4) Guest star: Elissa Landi

Speaking of Books (WGY New York - November 21) Guest: Elissa Landi talks about her novel *Women and Peter*

1942:

We Hereby Resolve (Mutual - January 1) Guests: Elissa Landi, Albert Einstein, Alexander de Seversky

The O'Keefe Show (CFRB Toronto - February 1) Guest: Elissa Landi

Speaking of Books (WGY New York - May 29) Guests: Elissa Landi, Eric Knight

True Story Theater (Mutual - September 30) *For Better or Worse* starring Elissa Landi, Henry Hull

Night of Stars (WHN New York - November 24) Guests: Elissa Landi, Monty Wooley, Jan Peerce, Benny Fields, Milton Berle (benefit for United Palestine Appeal)

1943:

Suspense (ABC - January 5) *Nothing Up My Sleeve* starring Elissa Landi, George Coulouris

Manhattan at Midnight (ABC - January 20) Elissa Landi stars in *Long Engagement*

Women Can Take It (WMCA New York - February 8) Guest: Elissa Landi

Double or Nothing (Mutual - February 26) Guest: Elissa Landi

Manhattan at Midnight (ABC - March 10) *It May Be Forever* starring Elissa Landi, Jim Ameche

Philip Morris Playhouse (ABC - June 25) *This Thing Called Love* starring Ray Milland, Elissa Landi

Waves First Anniversary Program (ABC - July 30) Guest: Elissa Landi

1944:

Green Valley U.S.A (Mutual - May 28) Guest star: Elissa Landi

1945:

Between Us Girls (aka Round Table of Romance; and later, Leave it to the Girls) (Mutual - beginning April 25)Panel discussion; Elissa Landi (Moderator), Paula Stone, Dorothy Kilgallen (note: Paula Stone took over as moderator in June)

Brownstone Theater (Mutual - May 2) Elissa Landi stars in *Mrs. Dane's Defense*

Songs by Morton Downey (Mutual - May 22) Guest: Elissa Landi

Mystery in the Air (NBC - September 6) Elissa Landi stars in *The Case of the Reluctant Lady* with Jackson Beck

Auction Gallery (Mutual - September 17) Guests: Elissa Landi, Eddie Rickenbacker

Blind Date (ABC - September 21) Guests: Elissa Landi, Curtis Thomas

Powder Box Theater (CBS - October 11) *Everything's Changed* starring Elissa Landi, Jim Ameche

1946:

Robbin's Star Time (CBS - May 19) Guest: Elissa Landi reads excerpts from *The Pear Tree*

The Playhouse of Favorites (NBC - September 28) *The Doll's House* starring Elissa Landi

1947:

The American Dream (WNEW New York - August 19) *Occupation Housewife* starring Elissa Landi

1948:

Author Meets the Critics (NBC - January 18, March 21) Authors: Marcia Davenport, Adolphe Menjou; Critics: Elissa Landi, Merle Miller, Cecilia Ager

Books on Trial (WHN - March 8) Author Mae Cooper; Critics: Elissa Landi, Babette Hughes

Annual Radio and Business Conference of CCNY (WNEW - April 13) Elissa Landi, Fred Allen

Studio One (CBS - April 13) *The Glass Key* starring Elissa Landi, Alan Baxter

TELEVISION
1945:
(Date unknown) Hour-long telecast from Manhattan starring Landi
1948:
Author Meets the Critics (Channel 4 - January 18, March 21) Authors: Marcia Davenport, Adolphe Menjou; Critics: Elissa Landi, Merle Miller, Cecilia Ager (Note: simultaneously broadcast on radio)

Note: A television script for *The Elissa Landi Show* was submitted by Video Associates Inc. (VAI) for copyright confirmation on February 2, 1948. VAI scriptwriter/editor Joan C. Usoskin, a former news writer for CBS, prepared the submission.

AUTHOR
1926:
Neilsen (London: Nash & Grayson)

1929:
The Helmers (London: Chatto & Windus)

1932:
House for Sale (London: Chatto & Windus)

1934:
The Ancestor (New York: Doubleday, Doran)

1941:
Women and Peter (New York: Alliance)

1944:
The Pear Tree (Chicago - New York: Ziff-Davis)

Photo Credits

Front Cover: Filmstrip images from top to bottom: *The Sign of the Cross* (Paramount), *Enter Madame* with Cary Grant (Paramount), *The Amateur Gentleman* (Criterion) with Douglas Fairbanks Jr., *The Count of Monte Cristo* (United Artists), *The Warrior's Husband* (Fox)

233

Back Cover: *The Sign of the Cross* (Paramount) with Cecil B. DeMille and Fredric March, *The Count of Monte Cristo* (United Artists) with Robert Donat, 1928 portrait of Elissa Landi by Howard Somerville, *Movies* (May 1931), Hollywood Walk of Fame (1960), 1934 book signing for *The Ancestors*

About the Author

Scott O'Brien has paid tribute to seven other deserving film legends, who had never had full-fledged biographies: Kay Francis, Virginia Bruce, Ann Harding, Ruth Chatterton, Sylvia Sidney, George Brent, and Herbert Marshall. Scott has contributed numerous articles for publications such as *Films of the Golden Age*, *Classic Images*, and *Filmfax*. His guest appearances include the San Francisco Silent Film Festival, Cinecon, KRCB's *Outbeat Radio* and *A Novel Idea*, as well as Jan Wahl's "Inside Entertainment" for KRON-TV in San Francisco.

Scott introduced the film classics *Trouble in Paradise* (1932) and *Double Harness* (1933) at the Library of Congress's Packard Theater in Culpeper, Va. He has also appeared in two film documentaries: *Queer Icon – the Cult of Bette Davis* (2009) and *Reabhloidithe Hollywood* (2013) chronicling the career of George Brent, a former dispatcher for the IRA. Scott lives with his husband Joel Bellagio in Sonoma County. (website: www.scottobrienauthor.com)

Endnotes

Chapter 1

1 Joseph A. Lubben, "Elissa Landi, Bluest of Hollywood's Bluebloods," *Dallas Morning News*, December 13, 1931

2 Jessie Henderson, "New Talkie Star Discusses Hungarian Goulash," *Springfield Republican*, November 23, 1930

3 "Without Nationality," *Variety*, November 24, 1931

4 Edith Hay, "Movie Star Landi Prefers Writing to Acting on Screen," *North Shore Daily Journal*, July 2, 1938

5 "Miss Landi's Days are Full Ones," *Daily Nonpareil*, February 27, 1941

6 U.S. Naturalization Records #72296 (July 10, 1935) lists Elissa's race as "Austrian" and nationality as "Italian."

U.S. Naturalization Records #309268 (May 10, 1938), a reapplication, lists her race as "Italian-North."

7 Hale Horton, "Elissa Landi's own story about her Grandmother Empress Elizabeth," *Movie Classic* (April 1932)

8 High-Life Almanach (Austria)-This Austrian publication listed Richard Kuhnelt as a Dragoon Lieutenant. Published in 1913, it lists Kuhnelt's wife as the former Karoline Franziska Kaiser (Austrian). The reference also refers to his having lived in Kleinhart, Austria, which Caroline mentioned in *The Secret of an Empress*.

9 Martin A. Kelly, "Elissa Landi: Deposed Queen of the Movies," *Classic Images*, October 1999

10 Lee Shippey, "Elissa Landi, Actress, Wrote Her First Novel at Age of 15," *Milwaukee Journal*, July 6, 1934

11 George Schaffer, "Elissa Landi Proud of Seashore Home," *Arkansas Gazette*, June 10, 1935 (Note: Caroline was signing documents (1910-11) as Caroline Francis Kuhnelt. Francis being a variation of her middle name Franziska)

12 "Amazing Elissa Landi's Travels," *Milwaukee Journal*, October 20, 1939

13 "Granddaughter of Empress is Stage Success," *Buffalo Express*, June 15, 1924

14 Romney Scott, "Through Seven Talents," *Picture Play* (April 1931)

15 Elissa Landi, "Put Marriage Back on Its Feet!" *Omaha World-Herald*, March 11, 1934

16 Border Crossing Manifest, Calexico, California (1936) Landi lists his age as 60, his race as Italian, and his place of birth as Dardanelles, Turkey. Suki Landi Sennett was under the impression that Zanardi-Landi was born in Piacsenza, Italy. A 1911 document lists his birthplace as Cosenza, Italy.

17 *British Columbia Gazette*, December 19, 1910, and March 9, 1911

18 Countess Zanardi Landi, *The Secret of An Empress*, Jean Wick (New York), c. 1914, pg. 258

19 U.S. Department of Justice, Form N-315 #136590 (June 6, 1949)

20 Passenger list. Departure from Naples. Arrival in New York on the *SS Cretic* (December 2, 1906) Charles Zanardi-Landi, age 30

21 "Amazing Elissa Landi's Travels," *Milwaukee Journal*, October 20, 1939 (Zanardi Bridge, near Prince Rupert, was completed in 1910-a railway construction project in which the Count was involved)

22 Countess Zanardi Landi, *The Secret of An Empress*, Jean Wick (New York), c. 1914, pg. 259

23 Countess Zanardi Landi, *The Secret of An Empress*, Jean Wick (New York), c. 1914, pg. 259

24 Countess Zanardi Landi, *The Secret of An Empress*, Jean Wick (New York), c. 1914, pg. 1 (Note: When Caroline died in 1935, obits indicated that her birth year could have been anywhere from 1874-1882)

25 Christopher McIntosh, *The Swan King: Ludwig II of Bavaria*, Allen Lane c. 1982 (Chapter 15 "Forbidden Longings")

26 "An Empress's Daughter," *Truth* (Australia), May 4, 1913

27 "Nurse Killed. Children's Miraculous Escape," *Nottingham Journal*, February 28, 1913 (At this juncture the Landi family was living in the vicinity of Leinster Gardens, London)

28 Church of England Marriages, 1754-1932, page 134 (They resided in Westminster)

29 *The Academy and Literature* review, December 19, 1914, pg. 525

30 *The New York Sun* review, April 11, 1915

31 Nellie Ryan, *My Years at the Austrian Court*, John Lane (London), c. 1915, pg. 57

32 Katherine Albert, "Granddaughter of an Empress," *Photoplay*, September 1931

33 Gladys Hall, "Every Actress Should Have a Child, Says Elissa Landi," *Motion Picture* (December 1932)

34 Lee Shippey, "Elissa Landi Wrote Her First Novel at Age of 15," *Milwaukee Journal*, July 6, 1934

35 "Granddaughter of Empress is Stage Success," *Buffalo Press*, June 15, 1924

Chapter 2

36 Marion Bussang, "Elissa Landi Gets Settled to Farm ," *New York Evening Post*, May 15, 1939

37 Angus McStay, "No Lady of Leisure," *MacLean's Magazine*, December 1, 1942 (Note: *The Digest of International Law* (1940) lists the Count's father had been a Dragoman of the Italian Consulate at Smyrna)

38 "Granddaughter of Empress is Stage Success," *Buffalo Press*, June 15, 1924

39 Elissa Landi, "Don't! In Four Languages," *Dundee Evening Telegraph*, May 23, 1941

40 "The Empress's Granddaughter," *Liverpool Echo*, May 17, 1924 (Note: toward the end of her career, Astafieva taught English ballerina Dame Margot Fonteyn)

41 John Gariepy, "Elissa Landi 'Wants to Live'," *Detroit Times*, October 28, 1939

42 "Attempt to Salve Lusitania," *Dundee Evening Telegraph*, May 16, 1922

43 "Quest for Gold in Sunken Ship," *Birmingham Daily Gazette*, February 1, 1924

44 "'Last of Britain's Pirates' Is Dead," *Plain Dealer*, August 3, 1953

45 Lee Shippey, "Elissa Landi Wrote Her First Novel at Age of 15," *Milwaukee Journal*, July 6, 1934

46 Romney Scott, "Through Seven Talents," *Picture Play* (April 1931)

47 "A Fan Letter to Elissa Landi," *Silver Screen* (February 1934)

48 Angus McStay, "No Lady of Leisure," *MacLean's Magazine*, December 1, 1942

49 "Granddaughter of Empress is Stage Success," *Buffalo Press*, June 15, 1924

50 "Mail - Mustard and Cress," *Hull Daily Mail*, May 19, 1924

51 review of *Everybody's Husband*, *Oxfordshire Evening News*, May 28, 1924

52 Maude Cheatham, "Her 4 Fateful Moments," *Screenland*, June 1934

53 Mrs. Elizabeth McDonald, "Fifteen Years of Dressing Stars," *The Sunday Post*, July 4, 1926

54 James Agate, review of *Kismet*, *The Contemporary Theatre 1925*, Chapman & Hall, c. 1926, pg. 255

55 Abbuh Randlaw, "Elissa, the Elusive," *Broadway and Hollywood*, May 1931

Chapter 3
56 Angus McStay, "No Lady of Leisure," *MacLean's*, December 1, 1942

57 "In Her Mother's Footsteps," *The People*, September 6, 1925

58 "Miss Landi's Days are Full Ones," *Daily Nonpareil*, February 27, 1941

59 "Spending One Minute With Elissa Landi," *Dallas Morning News*, April 11, 1937

60 Martin Dickstein, review of *London*, *Brooklyn Daily Eagle*, October 25, 1926

61 "Countess Landi's Loss," *Dundee Evening Telegraph*, April 23, 1926

62 Jonathan Croall, *John Gielgud-Matinee Idol to Movie Star*, Bloomsbury Pub. c.2011

63 Charlie Rice, "Noel Coward's Fireplace Comedy," *Plain Dealer*, February 18, 1962

64 "Millionaire Put off 'Change'," *The Sun*, June 1, 1943

65 Brian Masters, *Thunder in the Air-Great Actors in Great Roles*, Oberon Books, c. 2000, pg. 145

66 Jack Grant, "Was it a Ghost that Elissa Landi Saw?" *Modern Screen*, October 1932

67 Mel Washburn, "Mel Washburn Finds Elissa Landi," *The Sunday Item Tribune*, March 14, 1937

68 "Rescue Thrill in Filming Act," *Shepton Mallet Journal*, April 6, 1928

69 Ivan Butler, *Silent Magic: Rediscovering the Silent Film Era*, Columbus Books, c. 1987, pg. 186

70 R.W. Burns, *John Logie Baird: Television Pioneer*, IET., c. 2000, pg. 141

Chapter 4

71 Pendarves, "Academy Candour, " *The Bystander*, May 23, 1928

72 review of *Sin*, *Dundee Evening Telegraph*, March 8, 1929

73 Lady Eleanor Smith column, *The Bystander*, May 15, 1929

74 review of *After All*, *Yorkshire Post*, May 7, 1929

75 "Olivier is Featured in Russian Play," *Seattle Daily Times*, February 28, 1932

76 Oliver Way, review of *The Helmers*, *The Graphic*, July 6, 1929

77 "The Derby - How Trigo Won, (London, June 6)" *Evening Post* (New Zealand), July 17, 1929

78 Larry Smith, Library of Congress, email to author July 7, 2019

79 "Elissa New Screen Find," *Syracuse American*, March 1, 1931

80 Vincent L. Barnett, Alexis Weedon, *Elinor Glyn as Novelist, Moviemaker, Glamour Icon and Moviemaker*, Routledge, c. 2016, pg. 160

81 Adolphe Menjou, *It Took Nine Tailors*, McGraw-Hill, c. 1948, pg. 194

82 "Actress Wins Divorce from London Lawyer", *Fresno Bee*, May 9, 1935

83 Gladys Hall, "Every Actress Should Have a Child, Says Elissa Landi," *Motion Picture*, December 1932

84 "These 'Children of Chance'," *Linlithgowshire Gazette*, November 28, 1930

Chapter 5

85 Dickson Morley, "Landi Finds Herself," *Screenland*, April 1935

86 Leonard J. Leff, *Hemingway and His Conspirators*, Rowman & Littlefield, c. 1999, pg. 136

87 Leonard J. Leff, *Hemingway and His Conspirators*, Rowman & Littlefield, c. 1999, pg. 138

88 Elinor Hughes, "Theater and Screen," *Boston Herald*, May 3, 1943

89 Leonard J. Leff, *Hemingway and His Conspirators*, Rowman & Littlefield, c. 1999, pg. 140

90 Alice L. Tildesley, "Things Every Man Should Do - According to Elissa Landi," *Seattle Daily Times*, May 3, 1931

91 Maude Cheatham, "Her 4 Fateful Moments," *Screenland*, June 1934

92 George Gershwin, quote in promotional ad for *Body and Soul*, *New York Sun*, March 11, 1931

93 Elissa Landi, "How I Met Charles Farrell," *New Movie Magazine*, July 1932

94 Richard Gehman, *Bogart*, Fawcet, c. 1965, pg. 106 (Bogart's brother-in-law Stuart Rose was a Fox story-editor in New York; Rose had arranged for Bogart's contract with Fox)

95 John Rosenfield Jr., "Reviewing the Reviews," *Dallas Morning News*, October 11, 1931

96 Constance Carr, "Fine and Landi!" *Screenland*, June 1931

97 Jessie Henderson, "Woman Director Must Battle To Keep Place," *Denver Post*, April 20, 1930

98 Note: *The Yellow Ticket* had four silent versions: (1916) *The Yellow Passport* with Clara Kimball Young; (1918) *Der Gelbe Schein* (German short) with Pola Negri; (1918) *The Yellow Ticket* with Fannie Ward; (1928) *Zemlya v Plenu* Russian version with Anna Sten

99 Jerry Vermilye, *The Complete Films of Laurence Olivier*, Citadel Pr., c. 1992, pg. 69

100 Bernard Drew, "A Chat With the Men Who Made Movies of the Past," *San Bernardino Sun*, December 6, 1973

101 email from Caroline Landi Thomas, August 19, 2020

102 Robert E. Sherwood, "The Rise of Elissa Landi," *Film Daily*, April 2, 1931

103 Hedda Hopper, "Looking Over Hollywood," *Chicago Tribune*, July 8, 1959

Chapter 6

104 "Talk of the Trade," *Bioscope*, October 14, 1931

105 Elizabeth Borton, "Hollywood from the Inside," *Boston Herald*, July 9, 1931

106 Myrtle Gebhart, "Sunshine Squad," *Picture Play*, July 1932

107 Joseph A. Lubben, "Elissa Landi-Bluest of Hollywood's Blue-Bloods," *Dallas Morning News*, December 18, 1931

108 Cedric Belfrage, "Film Stars and Their Foibles," *The Bystander*, August 3, 1932

109 Hale Horton, "Elissa Landi's Own Story About Her Grandmother, Empress Elizabeth," *Movie Classic*, April 1932

110 Louella Parsons column, *Detroit Sunday Times*, January 31, 1932

111 William K. Everson, overview of *The Devil's Lottery*, October 11, 1974

112 review of *Woman in Room 13*, *Kansas City Star*, May 22, 1932

113 "Elissa Landi's Own Composition Played," *Seattle Daily Times*, March 27, 1932

114 Lawrence J. Quirk, *The Films of Myrna Loy*, Citadel, c. 1980, pg.134

115 Myrna Loy & John Kotsilibas-Davis, *Myrna Loy-Being and Becoming*, Knopf , c. 1987, pg.62

116 Neil Hamilton, "Stars I Have Loved, " *New Movie Magazine*, August 1933

117 W. Ward Marsh review of *House for Sale*, *Plain Dealer*, March 27, 1932

118 Harrison Carroll, "Elissa Landi Writes a Book on Middle Age," *Tampa Morning Tribune*, March 30, 1932

119 Jessie Henderson, "Elissa Landi Finds American Slang 'Most Interesting in World'," *New Orleans Item*, March 30, 1932

120 Cecil Beaton, "Self-Torturing Miss Crawford," *New Orleans Item*, December 5, 1937

121 William H. McKegg, "Master of Her Fate," *Picture Play*, February 1935

122 Malcolm H. Oettinger, "Sleeping Beauty," *Picture Play*, March 1934

123 Louella Parsons column, *Fresno Bee*, May 12, 1933

124 Edward Baron Turk, *Hollywood Diva: The Jeanette MacDonald Story*, Univ. of California Pr. c. 2000, pg. 102

125 "News and Gossip from the Studios," *Motion Picture*, May 1932 (This article misspelled his name McIntire)

Chapter 7

126"Pure Hollywood or No Hollywood," *Cleveland Plain Dealer*, June 11, 1934

127 Mollie Merrick, "DeMille Discusses That 'Ethereal Type' and Puts Landi at Top of His List," *Plain Dealer*, July 24, 1932

128 Elsie Janis, "Elissa Landi's Romance of Two Worlds," *New Movie Magazine*, December 1933

129 Charles Tranberg, *Fredric March - A Consummate Actor*, BearManor (c. 2013), pg. 81

130 Cecilia DeMille Presley and Mark A. Vieira, *Cecil B. DeMille- The Art of the Hollywood Epic*, Running Pr., c. 2014, pg. 198

131 James Agate, "The Cinema," *The Tatler*, February 8, 1933

132 Sydney Treymayne (penname for Sybil Taylor), "The Lion's Share," *The Bystander*, February 15, 1933

133 Letter to Mr. Keene (editor of *Silver Screen*), October 27, 1933

134 Gladys Hall, "Every Actress Should Have a Child, Says Elissa Landi," *Motion Picture*, December 1932

135 "Vows Made Her a Recluse," *Plain Dealer*, May 10, 1935

136 Caroline Somers Hoyt, "Do You Want to Know Elissa Landi?" *Modern Screen*, July 1933

137 A. Scott Berg, *Goldwyn*, Knopf, c. 1989, pg. 223

138 Forman Brown, *Better Angel*, Alyson Books, (c.2000) Brown's Afterword was written in January 1995. He was a founding member of Turnabout Theatre in Los Angeles, a popular venue for marionette puppeteers.

139 Richard Barrios, *Screened Out*, Routledge, c. 2003, pg. 102 (Barrios indicates that *Variety* reported that "the panze scenes" had been trimmed after filming was complete)

140 Joseph McBride, *Searching for John Ford*, Univ. Press of Mississippi, c. 2011 (Hepburn opted for a scene from *The Animal Kingdom* when Ford tested her for Fox's *The Warrior's Husband*. The test is archived at UCLA)

141 Max Breen, "The Screen's *Real* Mystery Woman," *Picturegoer*, November 20, 1937 (Louella Parsons' column from May 11, 1933, also mentioned the screening at producer Lasky's)

142 Douglas Fairbanks Jr., *The Salad Days*, Doubleday, c. 1988, pg. 197

143 Andrew Wentick, review of *Warrior's Husband* (March 16, 2019) Wentick is publisher/editor of Turningpoint Press - http://turningpointpressllc.com/

144 "Elissa Landi Charges Cruelty, Seeks Divorce," *San Francisco Chronicle*, May 21, 1934 (When the divorce was granted the following year, Landi indicated her husband's "repudiation" - "Actress Wins Divorce From London Lawyer," *Fresno Bee*, May 9, 1935)

145 Katharine Hepburn, *Me*, Ballantine, c. 1991, pg. 99

146 William J. Mann, *Kate: The Woman Who Was Hepburn*, Henry Holt & Co., c. 2007, pg. 561

147 Elise Janis, "Elissa Landi's Romance of Two Worlds," *New Movie Magazine*, December 1933

148 David Noh, "A Whale of a Romance," Noh Way (https://nohway.wordpress.com/), December 6, 2009

149 Hubbard Keavy, "Hollywood Chatter," *Daily Illinois State Journal*, May 28, 1935 (Keavy recalled this quote from Landi after he attended a cocktail party at her home, where she waxed enthusiastic about the future)

Chapter 8

150 Malcolm H. Oettinger, "Sleeping Beauty," *Picture Play* (March 1934)

151 Helen Burns, "Does Hollywood Want Me?" *Modern Screen* (September 1934)

152 "Courts Deciding Three Film Suits, *Motion Picture Herald*, March 31, 1934

153 "If I Were the Rain," *Offering to Eros - Six Songs*, (By Abram Chasins - Poems by Elissa Landi) J. Fischer and Bro., NY, c. 1933

154 H. Hanson, "South Africa Agog Over Reports Hollywood Plans Producing There," *Variety*, June 12, 1934

155 Carolyn Anspacher, "Movie Star Also Famous as Novelist," *San Francisco Chronicle*, September 26, 1934

156 Helen Burns, "Does Hollywood Want Me?" *Modern Screen* (September 1934)

157 Malcolm H. Oettinger, "Sleeping Beauty," *Picture Play* (March 1934)

158 Elissa Landi, "Does Music Help the Actor?" *Etude*, September 1945

159 James Robert Parish and William T. Leonard, *Hollywood Players*, Arlington House, c. 1976, p. 341

160 Dorothy Hope, "We Want Donat," *Picture Play* (May 1935)

161 Skype conversation with Caroline Thomas, August 6, 2020

162 Kenneth Barrow, *Mr. Chips - The Life of Robert Donat*, Methuen, c. 1985, pg. 68-69

163 Katherine Hill, "Elissa Landi Objects to 'Intellectual' Label," *San Francisco Chronicle*, September 30, 1934

164 William H. McKegg, "Master of Her Fate," *Picture Play* (February 1935)

165 "Theatrical Agency Wins Suit from Elissa Landi," *Sacramento Bee*, August 3, 1934

166 "'Snooty Elissa Giggles with Rest in Court," *San Francisco Chronicle*, August 2, 1934

167 *Variety*, August 14, 1934

168 Weston East, "Here's Hollywood," *Screenland*, December 1934

169 Nancy Nelson, Evenings With Cary Grant, Citadel, c. 2002, pg. 77

170 George H. Beal, "Hospital Treats Cary Grant, Star of Films, Who Denies Death Try," *Berkeley Daily Gazette*, October 5, 1934

171 Geoff Gehman, Down But Not Quite Out in Holloweird: A Documentary in Letters of Eric Knight, Scarecrow, c. 1998, pg. 113

172 "Actress Wins Divorce From London Lawyer," *Fresno Bee*, May 9, 1935

173 U.S. WWII (1942) Draft Registration - lists O'Connor's birth as November 10, 1884. O'Connor, born in Ontario Canada, qualified on the form that his parents "lived in the Dakota Territory before I was born."

174 Jack Grant, "I've Never Been a Kept Woman," *Movie Mirror* (August 1934)

Chapter 9

175 Jimmie Fidler column, *State Times Advocate*, April 16, 1938

176 George Shaffer, "Elissa Landi Proud of Seashore Home" *Arkansas Gazette,* June 10, 1935

177 Elissa Landi, "Does Music Help the Actor," *Etude*, September 1945

178 "Salesman's 40,000 Miles a Year," *Buck's Herald*, January 4, 1935

179 "Too Happy for Marriage," *Nottingham Evening Post*, June 4, 1935

180 Dan Thomas, "Meet Hollywood's Most Versatile Woman," *Anniston Star*, June 15, 1935

181 "Local Club Hears Actress-Novelist," *Springfield Republican*, December 17, 1937

182 Graham Greene, review of *Koenigsmark*, *The Spectator*, January 24, 1936

183 James Bawden, *Conversations with Classic Film Stars*, Univ. Press of Kentucky, c. 2016, pg. 99

184 Douglas Fairbanks Jr., *The Salad Days*, Doubleday, c. 1988, pg. 250

185 "Romance with Fairbanks? 'Rubbish' to Elissa Landi," *Milwaukee Journal Sentinel*, November 27, 1935

186 "Miss Elissa Landi," *Hartlepool Northern Daily Mail*, November 18, 1935

187 Conversation with Suki Landi Sennett, April 29, 2020

188 email from Suki Landi Sennett, May 7, 2020

189 "Elissa Landi," *Motion Picture Studio Insider*, January 1937

190 James Bawden, *Conversations with Classic Film Stars*, Univ. Press of Kentucky, c. 2016, pg. 100

191 Amelia Fry, Interview with Cornelia Bell Flavin Palms (Dec. 3, 1977), *Helen Gahagan Douglas Project*, Regents of the Univ. of California, c. 1981

192 James Bawden, *Conversations with Classic Film Stars*, (1980 interview) Univ. Pr. of Kentucky, c. 2016, pg. 83

193 *What Becomes of the Children?* is on Youtube. Both exterior and interior shots of The Cloisters are seen in the early portions of the film.

194 Geoff Gehman, Eric Knight, *Down But Not Quite Out in Hollow-weird*, Scarecrow Pr., c. 1998, pg. 115

195 Inez Wallace, "Elissa Landi May Marry Nino," *Plain Dealer*, October 17, 1937

196 Mildred Mastin, "Down With Romance!" *Radio Stars*, February 1937

197 Henry Sutherland, "Hollywood Chatter," *State*, September 28, 1936

Chapter 10

198 Mark A. Vieira, *Irving Thalberg: Boy Wonder to Producer Prince*, Univ. of California Pr., c. 2009, pg. 241

199 Graham Greene, review of *After the Thin Man*, *The Spectator*, April 9, 1937

200 Inez Wallace, "Elissa Landi May Marry Nino," *Cleveland Plain Dealer*, October 17, 1937 (This interview took place earlier in 1937)

201 Inez Wallace, "Elissa Landi May Marry Nino ...," *Plain Dealer*, October 17, 1937

202 Trade publications such as *Motion Picture News* began using the slogan in 1925

203 Alice L. Tildesley, "Dumb Doras Are Out!—Elissa Landi," *Seattle Daily Times*, March 14, 1937

204 Sharon Rich, *Sweethearts*, Donald R. Fine, Inc. c. 1994, pg. 181(various news reports commented on MacDonald's "sad but rich voice" - "strong, compelling voice")

205 Louise Mace, review of *The Lady Has a Heart*, *Springfield Republican*, December 19, 1937

206 Victoria Price, *Vincent Price: A Daughter's Biography*, MacMillan, c. 1999, pg. 77

207 Joel Eisner, *The Price of Fear: The Film Career of Vincent Price in His Own Words*, Black Bed Sheet Books, c. 2013, pg. 15

208 *Buffalo Evening News*, December 16, 1937

209 On November 19, 1937, Welles sent a telegram to Price, which read: "Have you conferred with that scabrous management of yours - We think you are crazy if you don't play Hammon [role in The Shoemaker's Holiday] and so do you"

210 Petition for Naturalization #309268, Court of Southern District, N.Y., N.Y.

211 Sheilah Graham, "Elissa Landi to Divorce Hollywood 'Completely'," *Evening Star*, June 24, 1938

212 Marion Bussang, "Elissa Landi Gets Ready To Farm, Scrub and Write," *New York Evening Post*, May 15, 1939

Chapter 11
213 Ward Morehouse, "Broadway After Dark," *New York Sun*, August 22, 1938
214 Jack Miller, "Landi Will Speak Here June 28, 29," *Daily Northwestern*, June 20, 1939
215 "7,000 Admirers Cheer as Film Star Kisses Martini," *Buffalo Courier Express*, June 19, 1938
216 Elissa Landi, "When Nino Smiles," *Milwaukee Journal Sentinel*, April 24, 1938
217 Hal Eaton, "Going to Town," *Long Island Daily Press*, March 23, 1943
218 Janet Robb, "Elissa Landi, Disguised As Self, Fools City Fans," *Times Union*, October 8, 1938
219 "Actress Says Plays Need Headlines," *Buffalo Evening News*, November 26, 1941
220 John Thomason, "Best Interview," *State*, November 13, 1938
221 "Elissa Landi Injured in Icy Road Crash," *Evening Star*, December 20, 1938 (Landi's agents reported the incident to the press on December 19 - some reports [incorrectly] stated the incident took place on that date)
222 John Thomason, "Best Interview," *State*, November 13, 1938
223 Welles had cast Joan Blondell as Lily, but opted for Landi. Blondell would wait a year before teaming with Welles in the Campbell Playhouse broadcast of *Only Angels Have Wings.*
224 "Amazing Elissa Landi's Travels Ended by Wreck," *Milwaukee Journal Sentinel*, October 20, 1939
225 Sheilah Graham, "Around Hollywood," *New Orleans Item*, August 31, 1939 (*Variety* reported that Landi averaged $400 per lecture)
226 Marion Bussang, "Elissa Landi Gets Settled to Farm, Scrub, and Write," *New York Evening Post*, May 15, 1939
227 "Actress Finds Ulster County Pleasing Spot for Home Life," *Kingston Daily Freeman*, September 9, 1939
228 Skype conversation with Caroline Thomas, August 6, 2020
229 Douglas Fairbanks Jr., *The Salad Days*, Doubleday, c. 1988, pg.345-346
230 "Nazi Warns Husband Of Amelia Earhart," *Detroit Times*, April 20, 1939
231 "Actress Finds Ulster County Pleasing Spot for Home Life," *Kingston Daily Freeman*, September 9, 1939
232 Malcolm Johnson, "Cafe Life in New York," *New York Sun*, March 20, 1940 (Landi's dance partner in the waltz competition was actor Royce Ward)
233 column, *Trenton Evening Times*, July 2, 1941
234 Jane Kennedy, "Woodstock," *Kingston Daily Freeman*, June 19, 1941
235 email from Suki Landi Sennett, May 2, 2020
236 Elinor Hughes, "Elissa Landi's Major Interest Is Nine-Months-Old Daughter," *Boston Herald*, June 9, 1945

Chapter 12

237 "Elissa Landi Makes Comeback in Popular War Production," *Ogden Standard-Examiner*, June 27, 1943

238 R.A., review of *Corregidor*, *Syracuse Herald*, April 15, 1943

239 Earl Wilson, "It Happened Last Night," *New York Evening Post*, December 24, 1942

240 Margaret Rose Thornton, Tennessee Williams, *Tennessee Williams Notebooks*, Yale Univ. Pr., c. 2006, pg. 359

241 Angus McStay, "No Lady of Leisure," *MacLean's*, December 1, 1942

242 Ray Peacock, "Elissa Landi Pays Four Income Taxes," *Richmond Times Dispatch*, January 28, 1943

243 Danton Walker, "New York Letter," *Philadelphia Inquirer*, March 3, 1943

244 Elissa Landi (as told to Martha Rountree), "Ring Around My Finger," *Radio Romances*, August 1945

245 "Cortland Social Notes," *The Homer Post*, June 19, 1934

246 "School Keeps for 7 Stage Boys and Girls," *Chicago Daily News*, November 27, 1943

247 Jay Carmody, "Miss Landi Recalls Ancedote With De Mille As It's Hero," *Evening Star*, December 6, 1944

248 Charles Tranberg, *Fredric March - A Consummate Actor*, BearManor, c. 2013, pg. 215

249 Elinor Hughes, "Elissa Landi's Major Interest is Nine-Months-Old Daughter," *Boston Herald*, June 9, 1945

250 Elissa Landi, *The Pear Tree*, Ziff-Davis Pub., c. 1944, pg. 137

251 "Elissa Landi Urges General Education In Talk to League," *Kingston Daily Freeman*, March 25, 1947

252 Bonnie Langston, "Legend of the Silver Screen," *Daily Freeman News*, November 19, 2004

253 Martin A. Kelly, "Elissa Landi: Deposed Queen of the Movies," *Classic Images*, October 1999

254 "Screen Star Elissa Landi Dead At 43," *Detroit Times* (United Press), October 21, 1948 (In his 1999 *Classic Images* article, Martin A. Kelly indicated that the form of cancer was melanoma)

255 "Prominent Persons Expected to Visit Elissa Landi Bier," *Kingston Daily Freeman*, October 22, 1948

256 "Landi Possessions Will Be Auctioned At 'Bright Acres'," *Kingston Daily Freeman*, May 28, 1949

257 Skype conversation with Caroline Thomas, August 6, 2020

258 Caroline Thomas, email to author, June 22, 2020, and August 26, 2020

259 The Real Gals Series: Caroline Thomas, December 14, 2017 http://hellogalbraith.com/blog/real-gals-caroline-thomas

Afterword

260 *Showman's Trade Review*, July 2, 1949

261 England and Wales, National Probate Calendar, 1976 (At the time of his death Anthony was listed as residing at The Keeper's Cottage, Crowsley Park, Henley-on-Thames)

262 Telephone conversation with Suki Landi Sennett, April 29, 2020

263 Skype conversation with Caroline Landi Thomas, August 6, 2020

264 The Real Gals Series: Caroline Thomas, December 14, 2017 http://hellogalbraith.com/blog/real-gals-caroline-thomas

265 James Robert Parish and William T. Leonard, *Hollywood Players - The Thirties*, Arlington House, c. 1976

Acknowledgements

266 Joseph Egan, email dated November 20, 2018

267 Laura Wagner, email dated December 2, 2016

Index